Randy and Tina represent a new generation of Christians seeking to
move beyond charity toward modeling a reconciling love
from inside their broken and bleeding urban neighborhood. Their
vital ministry in that community is part of a growing
movement of God aimed at the redemption of the city by the
strategies of relocation and reneighboring.
JOHN PERKINS
President, Christian Community Development Association (CCDA)

It's just very, very well written—a great book! The theology is on
target and well thought out. This will be a fantastic
resource for suburban churches who want to understand
and support city ministries.
I'm frequently asked by churches, "How can we get involved?"
I'll tell them, "This is a great book to tell you how. The
personal stories, the Bible study questions, the list of ways to get
involved—they're just what you need."
DAVID FRENCHAK
Director, Seminary Consortium for Urban Pastoral Education (SCUPE)

It is refreshing to see a book that documents the process of
relocation. I have seen families burn out trying to make the transition
into the inner city. This book gives excellent insight into
the process, and it demonstrates how to use the home and family to
significantly impact critical sections of the city. Randy White
has already had an impact on his neighborhood—but further, he has
influenced a large number of leadership people to
come alongside and join in the task of revitalization.
JIM WESTGATE
Mennonite Brethren Biblical Seminary

There is great need in our urban centers for the kind of proactive
compassion Randy and his family have exhibited by moving
to the center of Fresno. The kind of change we all hope and pray for
in our cities will not come without families like the Whites
and ministries like InterVarsity loving their neighbors one by one.
This book puts flesh and blood on the theories.
STAN JANTZ
President, Fresno Bible House

Randy leads us right to the heart of the urban problem—neighboring.
By his example he teaches students (and others who watch
his life) the power of becoming a neighbor among those whom society
has rejected. His ministry represents the cutting edge of urban
community development, a bright hope for the city in the
face of discouraging realities.
BOB LUPTON
President, FCS Urban Ministries

This is a great book. It is down-to-earth, filled with real-life situations
about the city. It explains how to get the job done that needs to be done.
TONY CAMPOLO
Director of Urban Studies, Eastern College

JOURNEY to THE CENTER of THE CITY

Making a Difference in an Urban Neighborhood

Randy White

InterVarsity Press
Downers Grove, Illinois

InterVarsity Press® is the book-publishing division of InterVarsity Christian Fellowship®, a student movement active on campus at hundreds of universities, colleges and schools of nursing in the United States of America, and a member movement of the International Fellowship of Evangelical Students. For information about local and regional activities, write Public Relations Dept., InterVarsity Christian Fellowship, 6400 Schroeder Rd., P.O. Box 7895, Madison, WI 53707-7895.

Cover photograph: Tony Stone Images

ISBN 0-8308-1129-X

Printed in the United States of America ♾

Library of Congress Cataloging-in-Publication Data

White, Randy.
    Journey to the center of the city/by Randy White.
        p.   cm.
    Includes bibliographical references.
    ISBN 0-8308-1129-X (alk. paper)
    1. City churches.   2. City clergy.   3. City churches—California—
Fresno—Case studies.   4. White, Randy.   5. Evangelicalism.
6. Fresno (Calif.)—Church history—20th century.   I. Title.
BV637.W48   1996
253'.09173'2—dc20   96-41456
                                                                            CIP

| 20 | 19 | 18 | 17 | 16 | 15 | 14 | 13 | 12 | 11 | 10 | 9 | 8 | 7 | 6 | 5 | 4 | 3 | 2 | 1 |

| 12 | 11 | 10 | 09 | 08 | 07 | 06 | 05 | 04 | 03 | 02 | 01 | 00 | 99 | 98 | 97 | 96 |

For Tina
God's good soil,
anchoring deeply
the roots of my soul
in what is real

Acknowledgments _____ 9

Preface ——————————————————————————— 11

Prologue: An Invitation to the Journey —————————— 13

1/ Flying Upside Down ————————————————— 17
A family chooses "downward mobility" and descends right into life.

2/ This Old House ——————————————————— 31
How the home we bought became one of God's workshops.

3/ Behold the City ——————————————————— 39
Seeing urban neighborhoods with new eyes.

4/ Love Thy Neighborhood ———————————————— 55
A way of living that makes love of neighbor not just a Christian ideal but a life essential.

5/ What's Good for the Goose . . .——————————— 65
What all parents want for their children.

6/ Like Working a Loom ————————————————— 81
We work with others at weaving a wholistic response to the unraveling of our urban neighborhoods.

7/ Songs of the City ——————————————————— 99
Real stories of hope and change.

Epilogue: Journey of a Thousand Miles ————————— 117

Appendix 1: Bible Studies on God and the City ————— 125

Appendix 2: 21 Things You Can Do to Love the City ——— 139

Notes ———————————————————————————— 142

Bibliography ———————————————————————— 144

Acknowledgments

First, thanks to my parents, who gave me the belief that I could do anything if I set my mind to it. To my father, who taught me to leave this world a better place than it was when I entered it, and who was always committed to excellence. To my mom, who taught me to get up from my chair and walk around problems, and who took wonderful space journeys with me at bedtime.

Second, my thanks to many other people who for nearly twenty years have mentored me to be ready for this journey.

I am grateful to Bruce Giffen, who introduced me to Christ and gave me a love for inductive Bible study. Lon Allison modeled leadership and an authentic faith. Doug Sorenson gave me chances to test my new faith on junior highers. Hillside Covenant Church provided these new relationships and a new family during my early years in Christ.

I am thankful to the InterVarsity students and staff at California State University—Sacramento, who were my early partners in ministry, and especially to Rick Pennington, I-V staff at the time, who taught me to love the Gospel of Mark and to love meeting with students.

I cannot adequately state what nearly seventeen years on staff with InterVarsity has meant for me in terms of Christian growth, mentoring and companionship. I am so grateful for an organization that has been as interested in me as in its ministry goals. Through all the Urbanas, fall conferences, student leadership teams, Bible and Life weekends, multiethnic gatherings, debates and prayer times I have been changed forever. And I am deeply grateful to all the staff with whom I have served in Fresno and nationally. Every one of them has helped to shape my understanding of ministry.

My thanks to those who were faculty and staff at New College Berkeley when I completed graduate work there in Christian studies. They taught me how to think, not what to think, and they freed me to love Jesus creatively.

Michael and Ruby Duncan, our friends in Oxford, modeled "flying upside down," and St. Andrews Church there renewed our tired minds and hearts during our sabbatical. Bob Linthicum, John Perkins, and Bob and Peggy Lupton have for years been literary mentors to me.

And my heartfelt thanks to all the students who have lived with us here at the "White House," whether for weeks, months or years. Each has played an important role in shaping this experience.

We give praise to God daily for our friendships here in Lowell—and for the partnerships we have formed. We are so grateful for Steve and Glady Morris, Kim Taylor, Brenda Acomb, Bob and Susan Engel, "H" and Terry Spees, Jim and Nancy Westgate, Jackie Holmes, Jonathan Villalobos, Keith Bergthold, Terry Jaurena, Joanie and Marty Martin, Bob and Kathy Macias, and members of the Lowellition and the No Name Fellowship.

Many thanks to my editor, Linda Doll, who left the hundred manuscripts to go after the one and shepherded it through the hedgerows of the publishing process.

Finally, for my wife, Tina, and my sons, Joseph and Jameson, I simply look to God in awe. Thank you, Lord.

Preface

Three things are true about our cities. They are growing at an amazing rate; they are fragmenting almost as fast as they are growing; and they will touch every human being living today in increasingly profound ways.

I have written this book for three fundamental reasons. First, as a chronicle of the evolution of a very average, middle-class family's transforming call to give their lives for the welfare of the city. Second, as a call for the healing of the city by the presence of the people of God there. And finally, as a testimony to God's love and provision for those who venture out of their comfort zones to practice a lifestyle of love in neighborhoods of need.

This is not intended as a sociology text. And though my assumptions emerge from what I hope is a biblical theology, I am not attempting an urban theology. I merely intend that you get to know my family, my concerns and the amazing call of God we have received to become a part of his strategy to redeem the city.

It makes sense for you to read this book if you find yourself answering yes to some of these questions:

☐ Am I concerned about the violence and signs of disintegration I am seeing in my city or on TV every day?

☐ Do I ever wish that it would just all go away?

☐ Have I ever wondered if God wanted to use me to bring change to our world?

☐ Do I ever worry that I've slipped into being too comfortable?

☐ Am I at all concerned for children living in poverty?

☐ Have I ever worried about the homeless of America's cities on a winter night?

☐ Do I wish I could teach my children to have hearts of compassion and skills in reaching out to those who are hurting?

These are some of the ways God has been molding our whole family because of our move to the highest-crime, lowest-income neighborhood in our community. I invite you to join this journey with us, a journey to the center of the city.

Prologue: An Invitation to the Journey

Planning on sleeping in, I turned in bed for the tenth time, trying to regain unconsciousness. Finally I came to the unhappy conclusion that I wasn't tired anymore. Murphy's Law. The one morning I could rise a little later, I didn't need to.

But I think there was another explanation. Something in my spirit was stirring. I felt almost beckoned downstairs. When I got there, in my bathrobe and slippers, the first thing I saw were the roses I had picked from our garden the day before; the first thing I heard was the dripping of a gentle rain that was falling on this Easter morning, falling on the poorest neighborhood in the city. And in the beauty of that quiet moment there came perspective.

The magnificence of the roses and the comfort of the soft rain somehow mixed in with the stark realities of this neighborhood of pain which we had chosen to make our own—and with the hope of resurrection which we would celebrate on this day. The blend was fragrant with the breath of God.

I thought of the children from this neighborhood who would come to our house today to accompany us to church. They, and so many like them who live here, need an infusion of wonder in their lives. They need to know the Jesus who brings resurrection, not only after death, but now, out of the often crushing circumstances they face.

I thought of the urban future that faces us all. Cities are relentless pursuers, overtaking and shaping the suburbs that were created as a form of escape from urban problems. Vast megalopolises are expanding all around the globe at an amazing rate, creating an urban world whose characteristics will touch every human. A San Francisco *Examiner* article, on May 26, 1996, carried the headline "Urbanized Planet Ahead."

I thought of our lives just a few short years ago—lives that seemed so predictable, comfortable and controlled, now changed forever as we embrace the problems of the people who live in the Lowell Neighborhood, attempting to partner with them in bringing some sanity.

And I thought of how wonderful it is that God could use such average, unspectacular people as us to embody his love among the poor, those whom Jesus designated as the special objects of his compassion and friendship.

All of these thoughts happened in an instant, sparked by roses and rain and resurrection Sunday.

*   *   *

This is not a book about "daring Christians doing profound ministry in difficult circumstances." It is primarily a testimony of how a call from God scrambled and refocused our family's values and mission. But more than that, it is a testament of a wonderful Savior who is helping us get a jump on the urban future that faces us all—and who in the process is bringing change both in us and through us. He brings change *in* us because Jesus loves the poor in spirit. For too long we have been spiritually malnourished, feasting only on the empty calories of this material world. Our hearts become impoverished, barely beating with the puny aspirations our culture feeds us. Jesus brings change *through* us as we seek to minister to children and families who have, by virtue of their poverty, very few options. This has always been his agenda; ministry to the poor is at the heart of the gospel.

I invite you to accompany us on our journey to the center of the city, to get to know my family, to learn as we learn. I am not in any way assuming that you are called there. Whether you are or not, the fact is, all of us who are able to read these words will see the growing realities of urbanization escalate dramatically in our lifetime. While not all of these realities are negative, as I hope to demonstrate, it is certain that our children and their children will face tremendous challenges brought on by the realities of the city. On this journey, we have learned so much about God, about ourselves and about life that we think you'll enjoy the ride and sense its relevance whether or not you are intrigued by God's love for the city, whether or not you feel called to relocate there yourself.

In the Lowell Neighborhood, a square mile devastated by poverty, crime, gangs, hopelessness and defeat, Jesus Christ is planting a rose garden, if you will, and watering it with a consistent rain. Neighbors will learn to tend it together. Perhaps they will become more than neighbors in the process. Perhaps they will even become brothers and sisters, tending the garden as one. It will be a thing of beauty, its fragrance and radiance bringing hope to other impoverished areas. It will experience what the Christian faith is best at: resurrection.

1/Flying Upside Down

Would you like to fly tonight?
All your life you have been learning,
"Every plan a way to get ahead,"
"You've got to build yourself a future,"
Those are the words my Daddy said.

Now there is another calling
Tellin' you to change your mind,
Tells you "finding leads to losing,"
Tells you "losing lets you find."

Turn it over, turn it around,
Down is up and up is down,
The world looks different to ya,
When you're flying upside down.
—KEN MEDEMA, MUSIC AT MARKETPLACE '86

IT WAS BREAKFAST TIME AT THE FRESNO URBAN MINISTRY PROJ-
ect, and the college students on this Christian ministry project in the
heart of Fresno's poorest neighborhood were staring blankly into
bowls of Rice Krispies, trying to wake up.

We had been there for just a week, living in a downtown building
owned by an inner-city missionary organization. The glamour, if there
ever was any, of "working with the poor" was wearing off. We had
painted rooms for a home for battered women, led a worship service
for the local rescue mission, visited inmates in the county jail and
helped build a house with Habitat for Humanity. We had studied about
God's concern for the city and seen our own concern grow, amidst
empty warehouses, broken windows and gang slogans just outside our
doors. Every day, around nearly every corner, we had met people in
need.

During this part of the project we were in the middle of running a kids' club for sixty of the poorer children in a rundown part of town. We were wiped out. Our cereal snapped, crackled and popped as we ate in the lobby of the facility, but not loudly enough to wake us from our morning daze.

Dancing with Darnell

But all that changed when Steve, the director of the organization, came in with a "guest" from the street. Steve asked this guy to wait in the lobby with us for a moment while he ducked into his office down the hall. Our students were somewhat used to homeless people by now, but this six-foot-five, two-hundred-fifty-pound giant of a man with filthy clothes and straw in his hair stood out as remarkable.

Loren, one of our staff, tried to introduce himself and initiate a conversation. That's when it turned weird.

The man grabbed Loren's hand and began to inspect it, as if he was an alien and Loren was the first Earth person he had met. He lifted Loren's arm in the air, looked at his armpit, his elbow, his fingers, never speaking a word.

Spoons stopped in shock partway to open mouths, the milk splashing back to the bowl. Half-closed eyes became saucers as everyone waited to see what would happen. Loren was a bit taken aback, and his polite introduction petered out.

Then the "guest" dropped Loren's hand and approached Ilsun, a warm and engaging Korean student who was part of our team. Ilsun instinctively held out his hand (realizing too late the implications), and the guest grabbed it. But this time, instead of examining the hand, he looked Ilsun straight in the eye, their faces just a few inches apart, and in a very slow and earthy voice pronounced the letter *D* as if it held great meaning. You could feel the tension rise in the room as everyone wondered what on earth this meant and what Ilsun was going to do.

Then the man grabbed Ilsun's other hand and began a strange, slow-motion dance with him, their arms entwining like vines around a tree. Some of the InterVarsity staff present were thinking, *Oh, no, this is going to be too much for some of our younger students.* The guest repeated his earthy pronunciation of the letter *D*. Ilsun swallowed hard.

Just then Steve came out of his office and, seeing this last encounter, whispered to Ilsun, "*D* is for Darnell. His name's Darnell."

Without losing a beat, Ilsun looked straight at Darnell and with a twinkle in his eye pronounced the letter *I*. "*I*," he repeated, "*I* is for Ilsun."

Gone were the tension and the fear, and in the time it took for Steve to accompany Darnell outside, there was building inside our group a slow and silent chuckle which nervously released itself as the door closed behind them.

We laughed because Ilsun had helped overcome our fear of the strangeness. We laughed because we knew that such encounters were commonplace in this neck of the 'hood, and as we responded with openness we sensed the presence of Christ in ways totally unexpected. We laughed because we were doing something close to the heart of Jesus, and even though the man's situation was cause for compassion, no one could deny the humor involved in Ilsun's loving response. And we laughed because we had shared this progression from intimidation to laughter together, and it would become a memory which we would retell and embellish as a group forever.

As I laughed, I thought how odd it is to be in the middle of such barrenness, in this urban wasteland, and experience such joy. How upside down it all feels. How surprising and unplanned. I had come in with a great sense of the nobleness of our venture—serving the poor—but instead I had been served. I was learning so much; I had been blessed by every aspect of our time there. And it all seemed so normal, so right that I should be there. I reflected on how this project and other forms of exposure to the inner city had brought me eventually to move out of the comfortable suburb that had been my home for thirteen years and live with my family among the "bottom" and the "least" in Fresno. My life had been forever changed.

Medieval Makeover

What a contrast it was to a time just a few years earlier, when I was floundering in a heap of mediocre dreams and details. After a decade of campus ministry, I could total the successes and failures of my work and find I had done no worse a job than anyone else attempting similar things, but for some reason I was feeling worse, even depressed. But these years also included searching questions about the relevance and impact of my work. I felt the need to get away, to recover and rethink. My well was dry; I needed to find a place where I could dig it deeper without interruption.

That place was Oxford, England. My family and I sank ourselves deeply into that medieval and majestic city, into the spires, the libraries, the lectures and the international friendships. We drank in both the tea and the tradition of our roots. I began to experience the ability to breathe again. And ironically, in that city which has bred and cradled some of the world's greatest thinkers, I began to relax my mind and simply appreciate beauty again. I discovered for myself what English poet Matthew Arnold expressed: beauty is only truth seen from another side.

As God brought healing and refreshment to my life there, I began to wonder if "another side" or "another angle" was called for in my approach to finding the truth of my calling, a calling that might evolve to fit me more completely. Maybe my assumptions about what life was all about, such as "building a ministry," "pursuing excellence," "leaving a legacy" and even "building the kingdom," were *part* but not the heart of my evolving call. I so wanted the abundance that Jesus promised, but, despite the fact that I was in ministry, it seemed as elusive to me as it was to most of my middle-class friends. Secretly I wondered if maybe there was a different way of going about "the journey" of my life and calling—a way that was simpler, more focused and clearly at the heart of the gospel.

A Family Who Changed Us Forever

Before long, a family from New Zealand moved into our international living unit in Oxford. The Duncans had been working and living in a squatter settlement in urban Manila, in the Philippines. They were on study leave and in need of a rest. We took them donuts, hoping to get to know them better.

I don't know what I expected, but when we rang their doorbell we were met by three very young, bouncy children. Their parents might have been fatigued, but these happy kids seemed no worse for the fact that they had spent most of their few years navigating the littered, stinking, violent slums of Manila. A strong friendship quickly developed between us, and soon we were exchanging photograph albums.

The contrast couldn't have been more stark. Our pictures were filled with smiling, well-dressed children amidst their toys. Michael and Robyn's were of smiling children too, but amidst the rubble surrounding the cardboard and tin shacks they lived in. Ours were filled with extended family, healthy and affluent, treasuring the grandchildren. Theirs were filled with Filipino friends, barely surviving, treasuring their "adopted" grandchildren. Ours were filled with the well-ordered, edged and trimmed world of suburbia; theirs with chaos, pollution and the ceaseless efforts of the urban poor trying to clear a space to raise and feed their families.

After a few minutes of viewing his pictures, I looked Michael in the eye and said, "You must be an amazing person, and your family must be an amazing family, to be able to do this." He responded kindly but firmly, as he had had to do so many hundreds of times before, "No, we're not. Jesus lives in our neighborhood, in the slums, and we've moved there to be with him."

"But aren't you afraid?" I asked.

"Yes, especially at first, when we would walk through the streets—before anyone knew us, before we had counseled so many of them in their problems, before we organized the community effort to bring running water to their street, before the programs to educate about sanitation, before the tutoring, before the church we planted; yes, there were plenty of chances to be scared. And even now there are times when we see the violence and poverty around us and feel vulnerable. Like the rest of our neighbors' houses, our house is made of cardboard and corrugated tin, and technically we are not 'safe.' But then, remember, Jesus lives in our neighborhood, just like he lives in yours."

He talked about raising his children in that environment, about how children value things like stability between their parents, love that is expressed, happy times together and new experiences. When these are in place, children are just as happy playing with a broken shipping crate as with the latest electronic device.

I looked at his blond and curly children bouncing on the sofa, so bright and alive, so like my kids; they were obviously *not* frail, hollow waifs, solemn, neglected and underdeveloped, as I had to admit I presumed the children of urban missionaries would likely be.

Flying Upside Down

Back at our flat, I realized something was out of kilter with what I had seen. Here was a family who had pretty well said goodby to the things most of the middle-class Christians I knew found essential. But—despite being fatigued and needing some vacation time—they were experiencing abundance and a sense of significance that I knew I lacked.

Their life and personalities didn't fit the profile I had created for types like them. Folks who live in slums on purpose, who not only minister to the poor but also partner with them, ought to look like Mother Teresa. When they're too much like me it's confusing and threatening. It was as if this family were flying upside down through the heavy traffic of culture, where mass media and secular opinions, like 767s and hang-gliders, routinely define what "right-side up" looks like.

They were flying upside down by bucking the trends of self-sufficiency and upward mobility. And suddenly I couldn't tell which version of life was right-side up. Was it my upwardly mobile, security-conscious, controlled and measured path, or was it the adventure they were on, full of very real dangers and inconveniences but full of fruit and significance as well?

When confronted with a lifestyle that is radically different, I usually do what most people do: I shrug it off. After all, I've lived my whole life in California, where people have progressed past finding a lifestyle that's an alternative to the norm; we're now into finding an alternative to the alternatives!

But I couldn't just write the Duncans off as being oddballs. They seemed like barnstormers, flying upside down while zooming circles around the more conventional ways of gaining happiness which we in the West have deified, such as a rising standard of living and ever-increasing leisure. They had intelligently, fearfully but faithfully chosen a yuppie nightmare: "downward mobility."

Something in me shifted. One could almost hear the gears mashing and heating up. I was seeing differently; my face could almost feel the push of the G-forces as the plane of my life began to bank into an experimental roll.

A 3-D Life

Actually, this kind of change in the ways we perceive reality is pretty common. It's the classic paradigm shift, where a whole new set of cues to what constitutes reality emerges and opens up new possibilities, new ways of seeing. This can happen with one's worldview or one's outlook on the day. It happens in big and little ways, but when it happens, we know it instantly.

For example, as I walked into a local mall in the city one day, I saw a group of teenagers squatting in front of a multicolored 3-D poster, staring with open mouths and glazed expressions. Some were clearly frustrated, their brows furrowed anxiously as if they were either the butt of a joke or too dumb to see what others were discovering. Others had the "Aha!" look streaming out of their eyes and were saying, "O yeah!" and "Oh, I see it! I see it!" and "Awesome!" Intrigued, I squatted next to them and for several minutes shared the angst of the former group.

Suddenly, as if somewhere in my brain a switch had been thrown, a three-dimensional image popped out at me, and I yelled, "Cool!" (totally embarrassing my two preteen sons, who were with me). "They're dolphins, and they're swimming right at me!"

A few minutes in front of another one revealed the sphinx and the pyramids, which would move as I changed my perspective. You've seen these new posters. They are a tangle of colors and shapes, and it takes a while for the brain to sort the information and make sense of it. When it does, *zap!* It's fun, but I still harbor a fear that some store clerk is going to come over to me after I've been getting a headache standing in front of these for twenty minutes and say, "That's just a regular poster; the 3-D ones are on the other side of the store."

Since I was a kid I've been staring at life, trying to sort it out. Even as a Christian, life is so "in my face" at times that I go cross-eyed. I get lost in the details, and it's hard to see a pattern, purpose or payoff. I've grown up trying to make sense of it all, waiting for the goals I've attained to lead somewhere, but too often each day has meant just putting one foot in front of the next to accomplish whatever is on my list. Is there meaning to be found in this pedestrian journey? Or have I been standing in front of the wrong life, waiting for sense and satisfaction to materialize out of the fog, like the 3-D sphinx and dolphins?

The experience of getting to know the Duncans and their life in the slums of Manila somehow shifted my vision, my way of seeing, enough to cause me to ask God if there might be a word for me in all this. There was.

That word was *mud.* Well, not just *mud,* but *muddy water.*

Our two families were both in ministry, but the Duncans seemed to have a sense of focus and a foundation, a sense of clarity about their purpose in life and the effect of their ministry, that I longed for. It wasn't a matter of romanticizing their life in the slums. Far from it. They were more than honest about the hardships. But my life, by contrast, was full of complex relationships in ministry, a needy and changing audience, nuances and subtleties which felt increasingly beyond the particular mix of gifts I felt I had. In other words, the water was fairly muddy.

What's more, I felt that the lives of many of the students I worked with were equally muddy. They were muddy with the competing demands of consumerism and with the alienation and loneliness wrought by rabid individualism. Their lack of confidence in their beliefs, bred by the relativistic climate of their campuses, was like miry clay to them. For some, the emotional paralysis and inability to commit which came as a product of their broken families had them stuck—unable to move ahead. Wasn't there a way for us to get a taste of the aliveness and meaning that the photographs of the Duncans' life in Manila revealed? Was there a way to connect both ourselves and our students to the sense of freedom we saw in them?

There they were, flying upside down, and most of the world was shaking its head at them. To the majority of my Christian friends, they represented a "daredevil class"—those who would do anything for Christ, no matter how foolish or whatever the risk. Their call was just another tightrope act, just another bungee jump from the bridge, certainly not something everybody was to do. It's easy (and necessary) for comfortable Christians to write them off. But I determined that if "flying upside down" was what it took to see things right-side up, then it was time to check into flight school.

I've always been both scared and excited by flying. A friend's brother took me flying when I was ten years old, and I was thrilled. He even let me handle the controls for a minute, as we banked around Mount Diablo in northern California. But I soon learned that to steer the plane was only a small part of understanding how to fly. Before he ever stepped into the plane, he had gone to months of "ground school" to learn all about the process of getting a hunk of metal in the air and keeping it there.

With our sabbatical coming to a close, I wondered what the process of learning to fly upside down would look like back in the States. Were there people at home who were doing what the Duncans were? What kind of adventure was I embarking on? Little did I suspect, then, that God was preparing us for the journey of our lifetime: a Mr. Toad's Wild Ride to the center of the city.

It's a Beautiful Day in the Neighborhood

Four years later my wife (Tina), our two sons (Joseph and Jameson, ten and seven years old at the time) and I made the move to the heart of the poorest neighborhood in Fresno, California.

We are a very average family. Tina is a quiet, steady person, gifted in the ways of friendship. We met in college, and our intact families supported our courtship and marriage. Our son Joseph is a tall, stocky,

curly-haired boy, a natural leader with a heart for God and a passion
for basketball. Jameson is creative and witty, keeps us all laughing,
and is the theologian of the family with his great questions about God.
We drive a minivan, go to the grocery store, sit on church committees,
try to make the nearly impossible soccer and basketball schedule
which our school district designs yearly, and eat way too much fast
food. Needless to say, as we moved into the Lowell Neighborhood,
we were diving into a sea of differences.

A startling 99.4 percent of all children in this neighborhood live
below the poverty line.[1] Only three out of ten adults have made it to
high school. The children of Southeast Asian refugees walk barefoot
through front yards that once were lawns but now grow lemon grass,
bananas and Chinese herbs. They round the corner, and as they buy
paletas, Mexican ice cream, from a vendor jingling bells from a giant
tricycle, they listen to mariachi music tumbling happily out of their
neighbor's window. They step around the glass in the gutters (which
doesn't get swept up by the street sweeper as it might in nicer
neighborhoods) and move to the middle of the street, where passing
cars tend to blow a clear path. They turn another corner and the music
turns to urban rap. The smell of hot links on their neighbor's barbecue
grill is a pungent reminder that life in this 'hood means that people—
different as night and day—are pressed closely together. In our neighborhood the population has grown by 38 percent in the last decade,
but available housing has decreased by 12 percent.[2]

Nearly a hundred years ago, it was the rich who chose to live here.
Now, despite the charm of the architecture and the majestic tree-lined
sidewalks, the children and grandchildren of those first home builders
have fled as the graffiti, the gangs and the crime increased. They
continued to move north, so that now, in a span of about five miles,
the street we live on stretches from the poorest neighborhood in the
city to the richest. It connects large homes crammed with several
families paying rent to absentee landlords with even larger homes, at
the other end, owned by the city's elite. The only people who are
choosing to make our end of the street home now are those who, by
virtue of their birth or their family's fall into this socioeconomic class,

are stuck in cycles of poverty, violence and hopelessness.

But God has called us to leave a suburban neighborhood which we felt was fairly stable and predictable and to live here in Lowell. And he has opened the door for college students to live with us, using our home as a base for partnering with the poor in the healing of the city. We have joined a small network of people who are attempting to fly upside down for the sake of the gospel and, in the process, are taking another look at life and God.

Read It Again, Sam

Taking another look at life and God means, at the very least, taking another look at Scripture. Juan Carlos Ortiz talks about what he calls a "fifth gospel,"[3] the one represented by all the verses underlined in the Bibles of Christians. It's the collective message of what we like most and most want to hear from God. It's the verses about God's forgiveness and unconditional love, his comfort and provision.

I believe this practice of taking only what we *like* from Scripture is the reason more people are inclined to use Matthew's Sermon on the Mount rather than Luke's Sermon on the Plain. Matthew seems more interested in the life of the spirit, Luke in the physical realities of life. Matthew says, "Blessed are the poor in spirit." Luke says, "Blessed are the poor." Matthew focuses on the psychological and spiritual aspects of Jesus' ministry, while Luke tends to focus on the physical and social realities of his work[4]—realities which make us shift uncomfortably in our seats if we linger too long on them. And so one tends to hear more Christians quote the text on the poor in spirit from Matthew, because hearing Jesus bless the "poor in spirit" is easier than figuring out what he meant in Luke by blessing the merely "poor."

This tendency to come to Scripture with a bias for what we want to hear influenced how I always saw Jesus' first sermon, recorded in Luke 4. It's the story of Jesus being handed the scroll in the synagogue in his hometown and given the chance to teach. He chose a passage (we know it as Isaiah 61) which began, "The Spirit of the Sovereign LORD is on me, because the LORD has anointed me to preach good news to the poor" (v. 1).

Now we rightfully focus on the fact that this is a messianic passage and that in applying it to himself Jesus was proclaiming his identity. And that is where I always stopped. But there are other messianic passages. Why did Jesus choose to read this passage? I think it was because proclaiming good news to the poor, binding the broken-hearted, freeing the captives, giving sight to the blind, proclaiming the year of release from the cycles of enslavement and helping the poor rebuild their cities is at the absolute heart of Jesus' message.

And what is the context of this message? A look further into the passage he quoted shows it to be the city (Is 61:4), that dynamic and bubbling mix of peoples, cultures, sinfulness and greatness, gnawing loneliness and mundane normalcy. Jesus had an urban agenda. He saw the poor, those he had just described as a primary focus of his ministry, as being instrumental in the solving of their own problems. It is they who will rebuild cities long ruined, locked into cycles of devastation for generations. And they will do it because he has come to live with them.

Robert Linthicum writes, "In his ministry, Jesus chose to move among the outcasts and the needy, he had nowhere to lay his head, and he was intentionally poor." Yet, "a strong argument can be made for Jesus' being born not into a poor but into a middle-class family."[5] This ministry was by choice, and it reflected a value which was at the center of his life and work.

As to his interest in the city, clearly Jesus had the tradition of all the cities of the Old Testament swimming in his head—their openness to God and their outright rejection of him. Jesus both pronounced judgment on them (Mt 11:21-24; Lk 10:13-15) and agonized over their fate. He wept over Jerusalem for what it was missing and what it could have been (Lk 19:41-44).

The Message of the Kingdom: How It Comes

If Jesus' redemption of the world was only spiritual in nature, having relevance for the brokenness of our souls but not for the brokenness of our lives, why this passion for the healing of the city? Why this vision of the poor themselves rising to build what has been shattered?

And why this identification with those who have always been poor, that is, the city-dwelling poor, those without the agrarian support structures of family and clan in countryside and village?

Could it be that Jesus sees the redemption of the world as somehow demonstrated in this new paradigm? *Urban poor welcoming a Savior and partnering with his people in such a way that the kingdom of God is brought to earth.* What an upside-down way to get a message across! And the message itself is upside-down to a world with a fix-it mentality, a world that says it's new programs, new formulas, new government policies and new jails that will solve the problem of the cities.

Down Is Up

So Jesus' first sermon was delivered "standing on his head," and the people had as hard a time understanding the implications then as they do now. Jesus was flying upside down, from the first words he spoke to his final, upside-down cry of love from the cross.

A few years ago I saw a map of the world which took me aback. It was published in Australia; you know, that country at the "bottom" of the world. I said, "Oh, look, this map of the world is upside-down." I actually felt a little annoyed. True, the map had been printed upside down from a North American perspective. But this map proudly boasted that this was the world from Australian eyes. Who defines what's right-side up in our world? As I began to read the Scriptures through the perspective of God's love and compassion for the beauty and the brokenness of the city, I began to wonder whether life in the suburbs was really paying off for us after all. Funny things began to happen. The rest of Jesus' message started to look upside-down too, but strangely much saner than I ever had perceived it to be.

So here we are, upside down and trusting, in the poorest corner of inner-city Fresno. And it's a beautiful day in the neighborhood, or "the 'hood" as they call it here. At first I thought, *No Mr. Rogers here, no sirreee!* But you know what? Mr. Rogers would do great here. He knows about self-esteem and relationships. And his message is just what the kids on my block need.

We're here! So what's it like?

Questions for Reflection or Discussion

1. Has there ever been a time in your life when you were asking major questions about your purpose and direction? Describe it.

2. What relationship might there be between those questions and God's initiative and leadership in your life?

3. What kinds of things might "flying upside down"—that is, choosing a radical alternative to the wider secular culture—entail for the circumstances of your life? Give an example of how you might live differently from how others expect you to, out of love for God.

4. Have you ever thought to yourself, *I'm not really someone God uses in a dramatic way?* Then ask yourself: *Is that what I really want? Drama? Or do I want God to use me in the fabric of my ordinary days to bring change in his world?* Spend a few minutes imagining how a life in the city might provide the context for that kind of ministry-service.

2/This Old House

I want a house that has got over all its troubles; I don't want to spend the rest of my life bringing up a young and inexperienced house.
JEROME K. JEROME

TINA AND HER MOTHER RAN AS FAST AS THEY COULD TO THE BACK yard, where her dad and I were sawing wood for a workbench, and yelled, "Come quick! There's a flood in the house!"

We bolted inside to find not just a flood but a literal waterfall cascading from the middle of our living-room ceiling onto the new carpet. All that was needed were some rocks, a mossy bank, a Bible and notebook, and I could have had a retreat there.

After shutting off the broken pipes upstairs, we looked at each other in disbelief. This was the second in what was to be a series of three floods in the house in three weeks, and we had lived here only a month. *"Save me, O God, for the waters have come up to my neck. I sink in the miry depths, where there is no foothold. I have come into the deep waters; the floods engulf me" (Ps 69:1-2).*

I guess it was to be expected. It's truly an old house. Built in 1904, it was originally the private residence of a man who had moved to Fresno in 1889. The original carriage house is still on the back of the property. After World War II, with the housing shortage in Fresno, the home was transformed into a boarding house. In the last decade or so it has been used as a boarding house and even a bed and breakfast of sorts for government workers downtown.

The first time we saw it, the place seemed huge to us, with over 3100 square feet, six bedrooms and six bathrooms (a fact which would later inspire postflood nightmares, waking me in the night with a cold sweat as I dreamed of all that plumbing!).

Two-storied, with a wide porch and twelve majestic Doric pillars welcoming visitors, it seemed perfect for use as a base for college students engaged in ministry. It has a huge living room, ideal for meetings; a huge dining room, perfect for the tons of students who materialize at dinnertime; and a study to house the InterVarsity office and library. The house is on Fresno's Historic Register.

All of these features combined to lure us into its magic spell. It was even within our budget, since no one (but us!) seemed to want a bed-and-breakfast-type residence in the poorest and most crime-ridden section of downtown.

The Money Pit?
We pretended that we were going in with our eyes open: we knew the house would need work. But we thought we could schedule the work to fit our free time and available budget. By the time the third flood hit, we had begun to get wise. But that was only the beginning of wisdom, as they say.

To help us conquer the growing list of problems and projects, Tina's father would come from out of town to help. (Dave Ricci is a handy guy to have around. He knows about most things that I never had to learn about, like electricity, plumbing and carpentry.) But every time he would begin a project, within a few minutes he would begin muttering, "Oh my ... oh my ... ," over and over again. It was really disconcerting. If *he* was discouraged . . .

And it didn't matter what Dave was working on. Invariably, a few minutes into the project, he would discover that he had opened a can of worms—the problem was a lot more serious than expected—and he would start muttering "Oh my . . ." again. From faulty or illegal wiring to termite-ridden beams to crumbling walls, everything he put his hand to seemed to shout, "Please, don't let this go another day or the family will die!"

Then came the smell.

We discovered it a few months later as we were working on some wiring which went under the house. Dave noticed that it was awfully wet down there—and *way* too fragrant. As I crawled under the house I was confronted with a lake that stretched over half the area inside the foundation.

And not just any lake. This was the lake from hell. Apparently a problem with our sewer had never been identified, and everything we had been flushing had ended up right under the house. It had been happening day after day, week after week and month after putrid month. Imagining how deep this lake was only made me feel sicker.

Wonderfully, a church helped us with the bill to replace ten feet of sewer line. But now, as I slept or wandered aimlessly in the halls, people swore they could hear *me* muttering "Oh my . . . oh my . . ."

I didn't know how many more surprises we could endure. But then winter came, and I found out.

Cold Storage

Large houses are great. They give one a sense of dimension. The nine-foot ceilings and wide rooms help a big guy like me feel like he finally fits somewhere. But as winter sets in, big houses with poor insulation quickly become like massive warehouse freezers. Our heating bill instantly quadrupled over what we had been used to, totaling nearly what our whole previous house payment had been. The irony of it was that, even with all the heaters turned on, you could see your breath in our house day and night.

We were freezing, and no one wanted to be there: not our children and not our students. Ministry was nonexistent. Knowing I had to do something, I had the house appraised for insulation and—even without the money in hand—ordered it done.

To my amazement, in the mail the very next day I received a check from a church saying, "Just thinking of you this time of year, and guessed you could use some extra cash." It was for the *exact amount* that the installer had charged me. The church had no way of knowing. Later that month, some relatives who stayed with us handed us a check to pay for a gas heater for the main part of the house. God's faithfulness leapt out at us, startled us even, with its timeliness.

Move Over, Bob Vila

Over the next several months, one circumstance like this after another led us to a growing awareness that God himself was in charge of the renovation of this old house.

We learned that he is pretty experienced at it. As problems arose, he mobilized many more people than we could count to adopt us as their project. Churches sent groups to paint the exterior; a local paint company donated over $1000 worth of primer and paint. Friends and relatives donated brand-new appliances (stove, water heater, dish-washer), replacing the rusting and dysfunctional units we purchased with the house, some of which had been red-tagged as unsafe.

The events that precipitated each gift kept us off balance and in prayer, but they also began to become means of increasing our understanding of the providence of God and the depth of the Christian community into which we had entered. The sense of panic which had characterized my response to each crisis was on the wane, and we started to have fun with the house.

A secret passageway which the boys discovered connecting two rooms of the house was fitted with hinged doors, adding fantasy to the space. A painting that covered a hole in the wall was also put on hinges, creating our very own mystery house "wall safe." The old pink candy-striped wallpaper was now a classy taupe, and the haremlike purple-draped master bedroom was now a tasteful green and mauve floral. These changes had begun to make the place ours, and, better yet, the life inside the walls was becoming merrier.

As in Houses, So in Lives

One of the most amazing revelations to come in the midst of that tumultuous first year here was this: as God was directing the renovation of the house, so was he remodeling the interior of our lives. We felt equipped to do neither, on our own. But through the remaking of this old house, "this old heart" was finding new foundations, hidden chambers, shabby, neglected corners and dusty masterpieces waiting to be rediscovered.

And God is into this stuff! Scriptures I had never paid much attention to started to make sense. For example, I could never understand why God was so detailed about the specific dimensions of the tabernacle, or why he would care whether the cloth around the tent of meeting was purple, or what purpose the embroidered pomegranates played in the scheme of things (Ex 25—28). But now it seemed clear to me that God, the creative One who chose the colors for the painted deserts of the Southwest, who routinely splashed the evening skies with patches of crimson, gray and orange—this God just loved how it looked. He's still looking at things created and things in process— whether a house or a soul—and saying, "Wow, that's good."

The Meaning of Homes

A second revelation came as we meditated on our first year's efforts in renovating this old house. We discovered a spiritual dimension to the process, with our house becoming a symbol for the shelter of the Lord.

In this regard, verses from Psalms 90 and 91 began to speak to us. "Lord, you have been our dwelling place in all generations. . . . You who live in the shelter of the Most High, who abide in the shadow of the Almighty, will say to the LORD, 'My refuge and my fortress; my God, in whom I trust' " (Ps 90:1, 91:1-2 NRSV). In some ways, moving into our new home—a home with a ton of major problems, a home situated in the worst of neighborhoods—was to us an act of "moving into God." He had become our dwelling place, the only unchanging aspect of our life.

If the neighborhood was initially threatening to us, if the house seemed at times to be coming down around our ears, God enclosed *his* walls around us. "Because you have made the LORD your refuge, the Most High your dwelling place, no evil shall befall you, no scourge come near your tent" (Ps 91:9-10 NRSV). God had not only helped move us; he had also become our address, the street where we lived. We were safe in *his* neighborhood, under *his* roof.

A home should be a shelter, a refuge from the tornadoes that can rip a chaotic swath across our lives. That's the standard line, and it's true. But it should be more than that. The psalmist calls God his shelter, but the context of the passage is clearly one of war (Ps 91:5-8). A biblical home is more like a battalion headquarters, a station where we receive the rest, the training, the support and the strategies of engagement which will enable us to live out our call to build the kingdom of God in a hostile world. As Rodney Clapp challenges, "Our call is to live not in private havens or retreats, but in mission bases."[1]

Our new home was perfectly situated to remind us of this. Perched like a cracking rock at the edge of a crumbling neighborhood, we live with the daily sense that our family life must not be defined merely by the routine chores of a middle-class household, or even by the conventional goals of privacy and the narrow, self-focused "family intimacy" which our culture holds out as ideal. What will make our Christian home truly Christian will be our "common commitment to a mission bigger than our family."[2]

So *God himself is both house and neighborhood to us, and we live in him.* Living with this perspective gives us a sense of confidence and security. And it keeps us mindful that we are in the midst of a grand scheme to bring others into his shelter as well. We've decided we will use our house, the relationships in the house and our presence in this neighborhood to live out this call.

God Is in the Moving Business
God has been at the heart of all the great people movements of known history. Human responses to wars, famines, persecutions and the

perception of greener pastures have all been influenced by his Spirit. "From one ancestor he made all nations to inhabit the whole earth, and he allotted the times of their existence and the boundaries of the places where they would live" (Acts 17:26 NRSV). God is the mover of whole cultures and of individuals. Israel was assigned a territory of great value and wealth, flowing with milk and honey (see Ex 3; 13; 33; Deut 26—27). King David saw God as the one who defined the boundary lines for him (Ps 16:6).

What is the purpose of God's interest in where people live? The passage from Acts continues, and answers the question: "so that they would search for God and perhaps grope for him and find him— though indeed he is not far from each one of us" (17:27 NRSV). Somehow our place of residence is intended to be part of God's design to draw us to him. From our experience so far, this is exactly what's been happening in our family. God was our Bekins mover; in the process he moved us closer to himself. But let me emphasize that it wasn't a totally smooth process.

In the last month before we were to move, an inspection on our former house revealed that the roof needed replacing, even though it was only six years old. We did not have the several thousand dollars required for this, but amazingly it became available through the intervention of a friend of a friend who loaned the money to us—and then asked not to be paid back.

The insurance company surprised us with requests for documents which were in a different city and could not physically get to their office in time to satisfy their requirements. But within twelve hours a new agent had provided what was needed.

Yet what threatened to undo the deal (and us in the whole anxious process) was the moment when the title company informed us, *one day before close of escrow,* that they would not fund the loan because the zoning wasn't right. After dozens and dozens of conversations with the city and with the underwriter, and after hours of anxious prayer, we stood in the middle of city hall asking the Lord who owned title to all the earth (Ps 24:1) to straighten it all out. It was important that he do this soon, we argued, since the people who were buying our house were moving in the next day, and if our purchase of the home downtown fell apart, there was more than a good chance we were going to be without a place to live.

During this time we learned things that no other circumstance could have taught us. In the space of twenty-four hours, two other families who had moved to the Lowell Neighborhood ahead of us offered to let us move in with them if the deal didn't go through. We wept over this practical demonstration of Christian community, something neither Tina nor I had ever experienced at this level before.

Then, like a mist at midday, the zoning problem evaporated—cleared up by an on-the-ball city staffer. My knees turned to Jell-O at the news, and again we wept with a newly imparted knowledge of the power and goodness of God. We moved the next day. It became clear to us that God was in the real estate business and was navigating for us the sometimes treacherous path to the city. We were learning what Emerson knew: "All I have seen teaches me to trust the Creator for all I have not seen."

It was a lesson we would need for the things we were to face down the road in our new neighborhood. This old house has taught us more in a short space of time than we can adequately convey. It truly is a very, very, very fine house.

Questions for Reflection or Discussion

1. Picture your life as a house. Which part do you feel has been most neglected over the years and most needs renovation? What room would you add, if you had the chance?

2. Does God care where we live? To what extent does where we live reflect values central to who we are?

3. Christians often assign a purely spiritual interpretation to the words we read in Psalms 90 and 91. But what might it mean to physically live (dwell) in the "shelter of the Most High"?

4. Where did you get your ideas about what a "Christian family" should look like?

5. In the family you are building (or would like to build), what role might a common mission play in defining what you become together? What are some examples of this, from your experience or the lives of people you know?

3/Behold the City

O N A WINDSWEPT AND RAINY DECEMBER NIGHT, BEFORE WE had made our big move—before there was even a hint of our having a part in "reneighboring a broken inner-city neighborhood"—I was driving through what for me had always been a sinister-looking part of town, on my way to a class.

My eyes scanned the road ahead. I was both eager to get there and mildly annoyed at this weekly nocturnal trek down this particular street. Before long, I saw in the distance the multicolored, flashing police-car lights that I had always associated with this part of town. *It must be a drug bust, or maybe a store robbery,* I thought casually as I slowed to gawk. Sadly, the environment of this neighborhood had deteriorated over the years, and now graffiti, boarded-up buildings, and bands of roaming youth had created the familiar images of intimidation that crowd the evening news and make us lock our car doors.

But instead of coming upon one more piece of evidence that the city was "going to hell," I was stopped short, slapped in the face. It turned out to be not police lights but the blue, red and yellow lights of a Christmas display blinking joyfully in someone's front yard. Its happy proclamation danced and reflected in rain-beaded windows and puddled gutters, shouting "Joy to the world, the Savior reigns!"

Why did I assume the lights meant trouble and not holy celebration? In every *other* part of town, twinkling lights had in the weeks since Thanksgiving meant Christmas. But on that particular road, I had taken someone's attempt at beauty and instantly assumed the worst. That small experience helped begin something in me. I slowly started to realize that there were powerful assumptions which, for most of my life, had been informing my posture toward the city.

The city is ugly; the city is evil; the city is dangerous. The stereotypes and myths associated with the city had become almost unscalable walls. This chapter is about a new way of seeing that gets beyond those wrong impressions.

Sleeping Beauty

The most obvious myth to emerge from that experience was my unspoken assumption that this part of town was incapable of beauty. After all, didn't the bars on windows, cyclone fences, deteriorating paint, lack of landscaping, and graffiti prove that the residents there didn't care about taking care of things? The place was so *ugly*.

Why is this issue so important to me? I was raised in an art gallery. As a child, when I would get a bad cold and couldn't go to school, my mom would give me a blanket, a piece of canvas and some brushes and put me under the cash register.

The smell of oil paint still yanks me back thirty years to those days. I was there as my parents chose the paintings for their gallery, as they cut the mats and crafted the frames. My parents' taste and aesthetic talent provided a silent and powerful stream of training that still runs through me. In stark contrast, everything about the city assaulted my eyes. This isn't a problem for some people. But my senses respond immediately to my environment, and throughout my life I have been drawn to those things which appeal to my inherited sense of what is beautiful. The city didn't appeal.

But I was in for a surprise. It wasn't until I had moved to a city neighborhood (even worse than the one I drove through that night) and began to meet our neighbors that I started to understand what I had been seeing. The beauty that exists in the core of the city began to dawn like a hazy sun in my eyes. It was the life of those neighbors that silently taught me to examine with different eyes what I assumed I understood. As one author has put it, the real voyage of discovering consists not in seeking new landscapes but in having new eyes.[1]

One family just a few doors down from us is a living symbol of the environment in which we live. As I came to know their story, neighborhoods I had been driving through (and condemning) now had an explanation. The Contreras family lives in an old house along with a few other families. Luis is a laborer. Each family living there pays more in rent than their modest space is worth, and it all adds up to a killing for an absentee landlord who owns the house outright, paying only taxes on it.

Their rent money rarely if ever goes toward improvements. Luis attempts patchwork himself, knowing that the owner will not. There are no flowers in their yard, not even a weedy lawn, for that matter, to suggest to middle-class eyes speeding nervously past that a real family with real needs lives there.

But they do. They have the same appreciation for life and beauty, the same human aspirations, fears and desires for their family that—in our saner moments—we all know to be universal. As commuters race to get out of this neighborhood, they will miss the visual cues that exist just out of view, testifying to the beauty that is resident here. They will attribute sinister messages to commonplace things and never realize that they have a world of things in common with the people who call this place home. Because most of those cues are *inside* the home. To see them one would have to stop and spend time there.

Bids at Beauty

While it is true that the vices and vulnerabilities of poverty surround

the Contreras family, there are vivid attempts to humanize and beau-
tify their home. They are simple efforts: the cracked plaster fireplace
is painted to look like brick; pots of flowers are hung from hooks. They
are bids at beauty; they are signs that someone cares.

There are other signs in the neighborhood that people care. Our first
Christmas here we noticed that just about every other house was
displaying Christmas lights, more than in any neighborhood we had
lived in previously. People here love to celebrate, to do it up, no matter
what the occasion.

But these are still externals. And if we depend on our culturally
conditioned understanding of what signifies beauty, we will miss
most of the beauty in the world. I would have missed the beauty of
a father—one of my neighbors—tenderly stooping to help his child
who had stumbled. I would have missed the elderly woman pushing
her shopping cart, a cart bursting with the reds and magentas of the
paper flowers she has crafted and sells along with her homemade
tamales. I would have missed the twinkle in the eyes of José and
Karina-Daniella as they come giggling to my door for a piece of
candy.

That is the real problem. Because we are all so well tutored by
culture to regard beauty as essentially external, we never get close
enough to people to see the radiant repository of splendor that exists
in their lives. And the poor are no different. "Man looks at the outward
appearance, but the LORD looks at the heart" (1 Sam 16:7). We need
to retrain our eyes not only to expect beauty in unlikely places but to
look for the beauty that reveals truth. That means I need to learn the
discipline of anchoring my sense of visual appreciation in people
rather than in aesthetics alone.

"What about the dirt of the city, and the graffiti that stays there
forever?" people ask. "Why does it have to be that way? What about
the trash on the street? Why don't those people take care of their
neighborhoods?"

We had all these questions upon entering our neighborhood. But
then we began to notice some things.

We noticed that it took three months for the city to fix a quarter-mile of streetlights that were out on our street. We noticed time after time that the garbage men did not pick up scattered trash as they loaded their truck, as they do in "nicer neighborhoods." We noticed that the street sweeper avoided certain parts of our neighborhood because the road isn't paved correctly. We noticed that the city *refused* to pave the road correctly.

When we saw all these things happen here that would never happen in a more middle-class neighborhood, we began to understand why the poor often do not invest as much in the appearance of their neighborhood as suburban neighbors do. It's money and energy down the drain. Their landlords will not "waste" money on paint to cover up graffiti or make repairs. In fact, the landlord makes the same mistake I was making. He too thinks the poor don't care about beauty. But he goes further. In his mind, beauty doesn't pay.

Both ideas have been proven wrong. We've noticed that when people in this neighborhood see that someone is investing in the area, they invest more of themselves as well. For example, when our summer project students have painted houses, it's not uncommon to see the homes right around them turn up with new paint within a few weeks. Major studies have been done of depressed urban areas that have implemented citywide landscaping projects; these studies have concluded that beautifying an area is a wise investment in urban revitalization. Hope breeds participation.

Beauty exists in the city. But just as a painter's job is to take the raw material of his or her subject and bring out the natural beauty in a way that enhances it, so also it is the job of those who want God to transform our cities to be willing to recognize what is already there and work with it.

God on the Mountain and Satan in the City?

If my erroneous perception of the city as a place devoid of beauty represented a barrier to me, the erroneous perception of the country (or nature) as "where God can be found" controlled my thinking just as powerfully. You go to the mountains, not the city, to get close to God. Right?

Harvie Conn helped me notice that every devotional guide I've purchased has a picture of a mountain or waterfall on the front. The message is that it's the hills, not the streets, that are alive with the sound of music. The sheer power of nature, which has the potential on different days to take one's breath or take one's life; the creative cry of the Spirit of God which we imagine echoing through the canyons; the fragrance of the eternal that we catch as we survey the world from atop a peak—all these drive us to look for God in the wilderness. William Penn, in the eighteenth century, expressed what many feel: "The country life is to be preferred, for there we see the works of God, but in the cities little else but the works of men."[2]

There's good precedence for seeking God in the wilderness. Jesus did it (Mk 1:35). The early Christians did it. The desert fathers built monasteries in the wilderness both to do battle with the devil and to seek a more holy life, undistracted by worldly cares. And for hundreds of years Christians have fled the routine of both city and suburb to seek the calm of cabin retreats and country escapes. God is to be found in the wilderness.

Some have fled not in search of God but out of fear over what they see happening in the city. Unfortunately, all too often the church has joined the mass exodus, removing the very salt and light that is needed. But the fear that causes this flight is understandable, even in courageous people. It's hard to look around and see things deteriorate. You wonder if everything you've worked for will be lost.

King David, by all counts a very courageous man, had this struggle. During a time of great turmoil in Jerusalem, he looked around and saw only "violence and strife in the city" (Ps 55:9). He described it by saying, "Day and night they [the wicked] prowl about on its walls; malice and abuse are within it. Destructive forces are at work in the city; threats and lies never leave its streets" (vv. 10-11). This sounds like my neighborhood. These are the realities that become the focus of the media and that terrify us.

They terrified King David too. Praise God that he shares with us his own initial reaction to what he saw. "My heart is in anguish within me; the terrors of death assail me. Fear and trembling have beset me;

horror has overwhelmed me" (vv. 4-5). No one is immune to the fear. It is an appropriate human response to a perceived threat.

David goes on to say that he is not only afraid but tempted to get out of town to his cabin in the country. "Oh, that I had the wings of a dove! I would fly away and be at rest—I would flee far away and stay in the desert; I would hurry to my place of shelter, far from the tempest and storm" (vv. 6-8).

David's gut reaction mirrors our own, but his actions show his character and his faith. He stays. What is it that allows him to get past the fear? He tells us. "But I call to God, and the LORD saves me. Evening, morning and noon I cry out in distress, and he hears my voice" (vv. 16-17). He prays. This allows him to keep perspective and place his trust in God (v. 23).

This is an important perspective to keep. The countryside does not have the power to deliver us from what we fear. "I look to the mountains; does my strength come from the mountains? No, my strength comes from Yahweh, who made heaven, and earth, and mountains." (Ps 121:1-2 The Message)

It is the presence of God we are after, not merely escape from what we fear. Psalms, so often the book of the Bible that best helps us process our fears, sets a consistently urban context for God's work. Robert Linthicum notes that of the 150 psalms, "forty-nine of them are city psalms. Most, of course, deal with Jerusalem, but some deal with other cities. Most are psalms that express God's creative love for the city."[3]

If "the earth is the LORD's, and everything in it" (Ps 24:1), we need to take another look at the city from God's point of view. Then we need to take a look at *our* point of view and see if it's at all similar.

I am wary of ways of thinking about the city which somehow give us permission to be unconcerned. For example, using H. Richard Niebuhr's "Christ in culture" discussion as a template for gauging the church's response to the city, many people adopt a "Christ *against* culture" stance. They see the city (and other human institutions) as evil and therefore unredeemable. Others adopt a "Christ *of* culture" stance in which the church, following a purely human Jesus, simply accommodates to culture and the realities of city life. Still others adopt a "Christ *above* culture" stance which settles for a mystical Christ transcending culture and standing apart from the pain of the city.[4] But if we look at the lordship of Jesus as Christ *transforming* culture,[5] we see that it has implications for both the evil and the good of the *polis,* for both the rejection and the transformation of city systems—and for incarnational forms of service, ministry and life.

These themes are amazingly abundant in the Bible. Ray Bakke points out that the Bible focuses on 119 cities in over a thousand passages in the Old Testament and 160 passages in the New Testament.[6] Some have noted that the Old Testament books of Deuteronomy, Joshua, Ruth, Esther, Ezra, Nehemiah, Jonah, Nahum and Daniel are developed structurally around cities.[7] Others have noted that the Bible begins in a garden but ends in a city,[8] and that we, like Abraham, are to look forward to and prepare for that day (Heb 11:10) when we all relocate to the city of God.

God Is in the City

We must teach that the city is "part of God's design, not just a sociological phenomenon or evolution of mankind,"[9] and that a sovereign God is in the midst of the processes of urbanization which we see sweeping the world. We are participating in his plan as we minister in the city.

We need to understand the city as not inherently evil in itself. It is an environment that provides greater opportunities for human sinfulness to manifest itself—and therefore greater opportunities for the gospel to show its empowering and healing relevance.

We need to see Jesus weeping over Jerusalem (Lk 19:41-42)—Yahweh expressing his concern over Nineveh (Jon 4:11), crying out over Moab (Is 15:5), weeping over Simbah, Heshbon and Elealeh, even "drenching them with tears" (see Is 16:9). We must pay attention to God's instructions to Israel to settle down and invest in Babylon, the "evil" city of its captors, and to seek its welfare and prosperity (Jer 29:7). We need to grasp God's vision for the poor rebuilding their cities (Is 61:4) and for the city being transformed into a place of righteousness (Is 62:1-12).

And we need to expose the church to the biblical call to take no rest and give God no rest—that is, to commit ourselves to pray for the city until God fully establishes and heals it (Is 62:6-7). Believing that God is already at work in the city, we listen to God in prayer and through his Word. We listen to find out how he is calling us to respond to him as Lord, as we become his hands and feet in serving the city.

Let's keep going to the mountain. We'll go there to commune with God, to be renewed and inspired. But let's go to the city too. There we will observe God at work, carrying out his transforming agenda. Both are important for getting to know him. We will be modeling what the Gospel of Mark tells us Jesus did in his pattern of engaging the towns and withdrawing to the wilderness (Mk 1:32-39), a pattern which ensured both his own spiritual equilibrium and the progress of his ministry.

But we will be doing more than observing God at work. We will be relating to God as he comes to us as a homeless person, an unsupervised adolescent, a pregnant teen, a "third strike" felon, or Karina-Daniella wanting candy at the door. Jesus said that when we reach out to people like that, we are interacting with Jesus himself (Mt 25:40).

Speaking of that city which for Christians has become the symbol of God's work in all cities, the Scriptures teach that it is given a new name. Appropriately, it shall be called "THE LORD IS THERE" (Ezek 48:35) and "Sought After, the City No Longer Deserted" (Is 62:12). God is in the city. And he is shaping it to one day reflect his glory. He's calling us to in some way follow him there to be part of the process.

One Strike and You're Dead

The third barrier was more personally disturbing. "You're moving where?" our friends asked. You could see the concern in their eyes. Almost nightly the news highlights the latest murder or drug bust. There were ninety-seven killings in our city last year; it was a new record. Crime seems out of control, and the city is in the grip of fear. Nobody here in Lowell thinks "three strikes and you're out" will solve the problem. It does nothing to stop the flow of new criminals who are now receiving their training on the streets.

During summer nights, we can hear the echoes of gunfire, from the pops of small-caliber arms to the alarming repetition of automatic weapons. Winter rain gives us a break from it. But on New Year's Eve, as revelers fire guns in the air, the noise reminds us of those eerie videotapes from when Baghdad was being bombed in the Gulf War. Everyone from the next-door neighbor to the police takes refuge in homes or under freeway overpasses from the bullets which fall like a hot, deadly rain.

"You're moving where?" they would ask, and behind the question would lie not only concern for our safety but something close to a threat. Sometimes it would come right out in the open. "I could never do what you've done."

Usually after several minutes of my trying to live down the nobility and courage ascribed to me, and after several more minutes of disclaimers about the city, people would be slightly more open to why a move there was a good thing for us. But I have known the feeling I saw expressed. It's the same thing I used to feel when as a kid I watched Evel Knievel jump some Grand Canyon-like gorge on a rocket-propelled motorcycle. I was impressed, but not enough to think I wanted to go into that line of work! My silent opinion of Knievel was, *You're crazy.*

Yet it was as we opened our minds to the facts of city life and took a second look at the constant stream of dramatically told crime stories that the daredevil nature of the ministry we were called to diminished. Yes, our neighborhood has more than its share of crime. But the nature of those crimes is instructive. The majority have to do with either intergang violence, drug sales or domestic disputes. The police tell us that if we are not running with a gang, doing drugs or beating our spouses, we are no more likely to become the victim of violent crime than someone in the suburbs. When we first moved in, we wondered if we would be targeted in any way. So far, we have been targeted only for the kindnesses of our neighbors and by a stream of street people wanting handouts.

As for burglary, yes, it happens. Some inner-city person (who appreciated beauty) stole our flower boxes from our front porch. We were saddened, of course. Tina's grandfather had made them for her many years ago. But we prayed for the person who had done it, and it was a good reminder to hold on to things lightly. Still, the joke in this part of town is "Most of the people who live here are poor, and there's nothing worth stealing. The burglars all go north to the suburbs where there's some good stuff!"

As time has gone by, we have felt less fear. People know us here. Kids wave to me as I drive, because they have been in our tutoring program. Our car is familiar to neighbors, even to the gang members down the street, and sometimes I wave to them. We belong here.

The *perception* of the threat that existed for a white, middle-class family relocating to this neighborhood was greater than the reality of it. Other neighborhoods, even in our own city, would certainly be different; more threatening, more "dangerous." But God, in his knowledge of who we are and what we can handle, has placed us here. The day may come when we suffer as victims in some way. Some of our partners in ministry in this neighborhood have been hassled, and various forms of crime, both personal and property, have come close to us all. The thought of what could happen makes me shift uncomfortably in my seat, and I don't like it.

But this place is a perfect match for us. God has changed our way of seeing the dynamic of crime in the city, and it no longer has a paralyzing hold on us.

If it is the fear of suffering itself that numbs us to God's call to the city, we need to get back in touch with what Scripture says in this regard. "Therefore, since Christ suffered in his body, arm yourself with the same attitude [the Greek word can mean 'purpose']. . . . So then, those who suffer according to God's will should commit themselves to their faithful Creator and continue to do good" (1 Pet 4:1, 19). Our pleasure-seeking consumer culture regards suffering as a painful disruption of life, an annoying distraction from the real goal of life: acquiring and building. It sees suffering as something to be avoided at all costs. But that is not the Christian attitude.

Are we saying that we somehow want to be victims? Absolutely not. It's not that we are to seek out harm. We are merely not to take ourselves so far out of harm's way in the name of security and progress that we remove God's primary strategy for reaching the city: his church. We seek progress in our lives, but we must do it with the intent of serving all God's people. We will never get there if we hide behind exaggerated perceptions of the city as completely evil, dangerous and beyond redemption.

With Harvie Conn we ask, "How do we change these perceptions of the city? We revolt against the definition of progress that feeds them. We take our towels and our crosses and discard our *Let's Make a Deal* way of living. Progress for the Christian becomes not a goal to be pursued but 'the unexpected surprise of a life lived in service.' "[10]

I'm Not Your Man!
Along with the fear of ugliness, the fear of crime and the fear that God was permanently on vacation in the mountains, there loomed the fear that I just wasn't right for the job.

At one point, about a year prior to our move, Tina and I were talking about relocating to the city. After working through it with each other and getting advice from friends, we decided that we were just not called to this work. Our reasons were logical: It just wasn't us. We weren't cut out for that kind of work. Our personalities and backgrounds didn't fit the profile of what a person would need to be to succeed there.

Was there any real chance of our creating bridges of friendship with those who lived in the Lowell Neighborhood? *I mean, think about it,* I would say to myself. *I'm a pretty uptown type of guy, when it comes down to it. I have advanced degrees. I actually like opera. And the fact that I could stand for an hour in front of just one painting is weird even for a suburbanite. Sometimes I feel like I should confess to being a recovering aesthete. "Hi, my name is Randy, and it's been three weeks since my last Beethoven/Vivaldi marathon." Could I learn to value, serve, care for, be friends with and love the poorest people in our city? What would they make of me?*

For Tina it was a different concern. We had known many people in ministry, some of whom had chosen to relocate as we eventually did. Many of those women seemed more outgoing than Tina. They launched right into ministry relationships, and their personalities seemed perfectly fitted for success in urban work, which we saw as demanding, chaotic, people-intensive and complex. Tina's most wonderful quality is reflected in a quiet stability. She has the gift of being a skilled and caring friend. For some reason we wondered if her profile would work in the environment of the city. We didn't recognize that the things Tina brought to the mix were just what our neighborhood needed. In hindsight it seems so obvious, and we are a bit embarrassed.

Eventually God helped us see that he was bigger than all these concerns and that our effectiveness was ultimately up to him. It turns out that we're doing fine. In fact, our neighborhood needs exactly those things that make up who we are. And, of course, who we are is more complex than our simplified characterizations. We bring more than those things, and we have been surprised by our capacity for adapting when we are intentional about it.

That is what Paul had to do when he said, "To the Jews I became like a Jew, to win the Jews. . . . To the weak I became weak, to win the weak. I have become all things to all men so that by all possible means I might save some. I do all this for the sake of the gospel, that I may share in its blessings" (1 Cor 9:20, 22-23). God has taken who we are, helped us adapt to our new environment, and mixed in some new material which he has brought to our lives and personalities—and now Tina and I marvel at how well we fit this neighborhood. Like Paul, we look forward to the blessings inherent in this incarnational process.

In this same section of 1 Corinthians, I have found it interesting that while Paul says that he became *like* the Jews, he says that he actually *became* weak. I can learn to talk with people with minimal education, learn to wear jeans instead of slacks, learn to appreciate mariachi music, learn to eat Vietnamese food without crying (maybe). I attempt to identify with folks by building cultural bridges. All of that is becoming *like* a people. But if I do all of that from the outside, then go home to my homogenous, predictable, insulated environment, have

I really earned the credibility it will take to proclaim the gospel with authority in the Lowell Neighborhood? I must *become* weak. In Lowell, that means having our flower pots ripped off and a car fire-bombed in our alley, experiencing gunfire on New Year's Eve, hassling with the city to get the streetlights back on. It means experiencing all of these things *with*—right alongside—the people in my neighborhood as they experience them too. We are weak together. We are in it together.

With this strategy, God can take any personality, any mix of gifts, any limitations and use them for his kingdom in the city. What I needed to do was stop worrying about how good a minister I would be in the city and just seek the greatness that is available to all. Martin Luther King Jr., in his own echo of Jesus, said it best: "Anyone can be great, because everyone can serve. You don't need a college degree to serve. You don't need to make your subject and your verb agree to serve. You only need a heart full of grace, and a soul generated by love." This is for me. I can do this. So can everybody.

Urban Malaise

The final myth I found myself dealing with is what both sociologists and the average commuter talk about: the drain of city life. At least one early urban theorist postulated that urban size and disarray contributed to a deterioration of mental health, "creating what came to be called 'urban malaise'—loneliness, depression and anxiety."[11] This fear presents a huge barrier for many, who ask, "Can I survive the burden of living in the inner city? How will I deal with the pressing together of people groups that are so different?"

But at least two studies, one by the National Center for Health Statistics, show evidence that city dwellers are less likely than their counterparts in the country to suffer symptoms of mental illness.[12] The *perception* of the emotional burden that the so-called overcrowding in the city is supposed to produce is worse than the reality. In fact, for many people in the world, dense populations are welcomed as a form of security. The children in our neighborhood are more comfortable being with others than being alone. As evidence of this, Harvie Conn cites an experimental program in Boston's West End that gave inner-city boys the chance to explore nature on the sandy beaches of Cape Cod. The program had to be abandoned because "the boys could not understand why anyone would want to visit, much less live in, such a lonely spot."[13] It's not to say that inner-city kids don't appreciate nature. But the vastness of it can be a bit unnerving for them.

A desire to be with others is a wonderful sign of mental health. And the desire for connection and interdependence is, in fact, a biblical value. Evangelicals like to give lip service to it but are often hard pressed to define what interdependence might look like in practice. Where is the evidence in the church today of actually employing this value? Rather, aren't we through our highly individualized lifestyles simply pursuing a Christianized version of the Marlboro Man vision of life? We are rugged individualists, answering to no one but ourselves, relating to others only on our timetables.

The common objections about living in the city—that it's crowded and noisy and fast-paced and impersonal—sound to me like a confession that we really don't trust God to provide the spaces we need for silence, reflection, relaxation and peace. We feel the need to create our own artificial environment where we control all the variables to ensure our emotional equilibrium. But that's a suburban pipe dream. We can't really do that anywhere, not in the country and not in the city. There are too many variables in this complex world. Our Father knows what we need. If we seek first his kingdom and his justice, all that we need will be given to us (Mt 6:32-33).

This book is a testimony that all we have needed has been given to us. Where once I had all the questions about the stress of urban life, concerns about my ability to focus amid the distractions, anxiety over how overwhelming the needs of the city seemed or how large the problems loomed, now I am beginning to see my heavenly Father providing the spaces in the day, apportioned at the right time, to provide care for my mind and my soul.

It's often through the interconnectedness of the community here that he provides. One of the other families that intentionally moved into the Lowell Neighborhood when we did brings by some freshly baked bread. Another offers a gift certificate for a quiet retreat at a city café. Another offers us their cabin in the mountains for a well-positioned dip into a more formal solitude.

There are moments in the night that are so quiet in the city that I can hear the low voices of the bells in our church as they sound midnight. Jesus lives in the city. He creates peace—peace like an urban river—wherever he is. "There is a river whose streams make glad the city of God, the holy habitation of the Most High. God is in the midst of the city; it shall not be moved; God will help it when the morning dawns" (Ps 46:4-5 NRSV).

Questions for Reflection or Discussion

1. What adjectives come to mind when you think of urban environments?

2. What feelings are you aware of when you travel through a "bad" part of town? Where do they come from?

3. In what ways might the city help you develop your relationship with God? How are these different from what you might experience in the midst of a "mountain retreat"?

4. In what ways have you envisioned a future that has as its main purpose to "keep myself out of harm's way"? How has this influenced your attitudes toward the city?

5. What aspects of your character seem most inconsistent with what you perceive to be necessary for success (or survival) in the city? What are some ways you could imagine God working through those traits?

4/Love Thy Neighborhood

∎

For what do we live, but to make sport
for our neighbours, and laugh at
them in our turn?
—MR. BENNET IN JANE AUSTEN'S
PRIDE AND PREJUDICE

In great cities men are brought together
by the desire of gain. They are
not in a state of cooperation, but of
isolation, as to the making of fortunes;
and for all the rest they are
careless of neighbours. Christianity
teaches us to love our neighbour as
ourself; modern society acknowledges
no neighbour.
—MR. MORLEY IN BENJAMIN DISRAELI'S SYBIL

We must love one another or die.
—W. H. AUDEN

I HAVE BEEN TALKING ABOUT A *WAY OF SEEING* THAT WORKS
through the things that cause the most antipathy toward the city. Now
it's time to explore a *way of living* which makes "love of neighbor"
not just a Christian ideal but a natural life rhythm, the kind where God
regularly reveals himself through us in the average circumstances of
being a neighbor.

Involvement: The Pathway to Neighbor-Love

As I walk on McKenzie Avenue at dusk in the heart of Lowell, a Latino
boy yells, "Hey, *you!*" at me. I've learned not to "get in the face" of
urban youth by staring at them. Sometimes even a misinterpreted look
can be provocation, in their code of behavior. I keep walking and steal

a quick glance. A shaved head with a rat-tail lock of hair on the back is all I can make out. I'm walking with friends, so I figure I'd better pretend not to hear, and I keep going. But "Hey, *you!*" sounds again, this time even louder, and I know I have to stop. As I turn, I see to my relief that it's Adam, one of the kids I first met during one of our urban projects. I am convinced Adam is going to be a comedian one day. He has more acting talent than any kid his age I have ever seen. I've come to appreciate his quick wit and his helpful spirit.

He'd forgotten my name but wanted to say hi. He is someone I never thought would have been open to my friendship. But Adam is my neighbor. Because we have had chances to interact, I know something about him that I love. It's Jesus with a rat-tail lock of hair and a joke at the ready.

Different day, same street. I am walking to our tutoring program, and another Latino boy, about twelve years old, is right behind me. He has one hand under his coat. I turn and look over my shoulder again, but before I have a chance to get worried, he says, "Hi!" and catches up to me. I recognize him but can't remember his name. I say, "What've you got there?" He pulls out a hamburger that he bought several blocks away and is protecting from the light rain that's falling. I mentally kick myself for having assumed it was a weapon.

He reminds me that his name is Xavier and he's Adam's brother. He talks to me for a few minutes as we walk, then heads into his apartment. I think, *How unusual that a boy his age would strike up a conversation with an adult. I really love how he took initiative.* Xavier is my neighbor. Because we have had chances to interact, I know something about him that I love. It's Jesus with a burger, wanting to know me, wanting to talk.

Juan is an OG. He is sitting in my living room because his wife Angelica is here for the women's night Tina is leading in the other room. They are doing a craft tonight. I am struck with how little space is left on Juan's arms between the tattoos. He has the potential to look very threatening, except that tonight he has the sweetest smile on his face as we talk about Jesus. What's an OG? It stands for "original gangster." Juan is forty now. Somewhere along the way he experienced the love and caring of urban missionaries, and now his life seems to be settling down a bit. But his reputation follows him. He was known in Fresno as a wild man in the gangs.

I watch him care for his two little girls, exercising a patience with them that I have never had as a parent, and my appreciation grows. He still has problems. He and his wife are on rocky ground. Both have a history of drug or alcohol abuse. Juan does not fit the profile of men I seek out for friendship. But I have seen something in him which I have really appreciated. Because we have had chances to interact, I know something about him that I love. It's Jesus with tattoos, demonstrating the tenderness of a father's love.

Shared History

I have told these stories to convey how love of neighbor develops. In each case the neighbors I now love are people very unlike me. There are cultural, socioeconomic and educational distances between us. We are worlds apart in our family structures, in the choices we have made, in the doors our culture opens or closes for us, and often in the basic ways we approach the world, such as our view of time, money and relationships. But the small ways our paths have crossed have created enough shared history to provide the seedbed for love.

I do not mean to suggest that love of neighbor is merely appreciation or affection. Love cannot be defined as mere sentiment. It is something more like muscle. It grows with each stretch. It toughens with each stress. But neighbor-love has to begin somewhere. For me, it helps to look for ways to connect with the person. Then the exercise of that muscle can begin in loving actions. Sometimes these connections happen quickly, sometimes slowly. I can't explain it, any more than I can explain why we feel "chemistry" with some people and not with others.

Making Connections

Whether it takes days or weeks or months, I'm learning that the key has little to do with chemistry and more to do with simple chances for paths to cross. Shared experiences, chances to talk—even things like buying ice cream at the same time create these connections. Then the connections can develop into greater opportunities for involvement with one another. This is where the initiative of the Holy Spirit is important. For me, the key has been to pray that God will orchestrate and direct this kind of neighbor-love.

But my purpose here is not to define love or even to describe loving actions. My point is that there is something inherent in the process of getting to know my neighbors in Lowell which automatically has led to love. Those points of connection have led to further chances to demonstrate the God of love through loving actions. This is important, because Christians have made love of neighbor such an *ideal* that somewhere in the process we gave ourselves permission to fall short of it, in the same way that we look at the ideals of self-denial and suffering as unreachable.

It is the act of *involvement* which provides the key to neighbor-love. It was, according to Jesus, the commitment to involvement that characterized the good Samaritan's neighborliness (Lk 10). It's a familiar story. An expert in the law has responded to Jesus' teaching on the first commandment—the one about loving God and loving your neighbor as yourself—with the question "Who is my neighbor?"

The question is a smoke screen from the word go because the lawyer wants to "justify himself." Justify what? I believe he wants to justify his own inaction by questioning how far his responsibility goes with regard to the command to love. In response to the smoke screen, Jesus tells the story of the loving actions of a Samaritan man who, as part of an ethnic group the Israelites hated, demonstrated what it meant to act as a neighbor. His actions were a great contrast to the religious elite who did not want to defile themselves and passed by the injured man on the other side of the road. For them legalism took precedence over mercy. But the Samaritan man stopped, got involved at his own expense and made provisions to bring the injured man back to health.

Jesus intentionally chose his characters in this parable to offend the religious patriotism of his hearers. Here was a man representing an ethnicity which the Jews resented and avoided, demonstrating a capacity to care which exceeded that of those people who were most supposed to care. As Craig Keener has pointed out, "Jesus' questioner would hate Samaritans, yet he is forced to follow the moral example of a Samaritan in Jesus' story. This parable forced him to answer his own question, 'Who is my neighbor?' "[1]

We might be motivated to go easy on the three leaders who passed by. After all, helping the injured man would have severely inconvenienced them: they would have to perform certain purification rituals to regain ceremonial purity after dealing with an "unclean" person. But the reason we'd go easy on them might be that we too (though we do not have the excuse of their offices to hide behind) do not welcome the intrusions of people in need on our lives. They are an inconvenience.

Love Is Not Convenient

Love of neighbor begins with the willingness to be inconvenienced. It means saying yes to God's right to direct people to us based on his objectives and their needs rather than our comfort and convenience.

Jodie, one of the students involved in our ministry to the city, has experienced how complex this ministry of inconvenience can be. In the midst of her week, juggling commitments to school, work and the relationships she is building with hurting people on Fresno's west side, she has learned to ask for God's guidance daily with this prayer: "Lord, let people get in the way."

Often the poor living in the city are better at open and flexible living than we are. Bob Lupton, a Christian community organizer in Atlanta's Summerhill community, commented about the people he met as he and his wife moved into that community, which had been decimated by poverty and crime. He was amazed at his neighbors' natural capacity to care, and he noted that it made "our scheduled, metered acts of service sometimes seem trite and even self-serving."[2]

Living in the city has imposed that "ministry of inconvenience" on us. We don't choose the times a single mom from the neighborhood comes to our door needing to talk. We don't schedule when neighborhood kids will come by to get their bike tires pumped. And it is hard to drive unmoved past the gaping needs of the neighborhood, unless one is totally hardhearted or suffering from a serious case of denial. There are injured folk on almost every side. The one choice we do have in the whole process is to say yes or no when opportunities arise to serve in Christ's name—when they arise because they arrive at our door or because we become aware of something not being right in the neighborhood. We are applying the yes or no not just to random requests for help but to the opportunities for involvement which the Lord himself is presenting to us.

An interesting byproduct is that love of neighbor becomes an investment in our own security and safety. The more neighbors we know and serve, the more children who come here to have a snack, learn about Jesus, get help with their homework or learn to read, the fewer the flower boxes that get stolen or windows broken.

The city is showing that it has a way of creating a powerful current in our lives where love of neighbor is not only a value but something as necessary as air, not an abstract idea but a muscular, almost gymnastic approach to service and human relationships. We are attempting to bend over backwards to demonstrate the kind of love that the good Samaritan demonstrated.

That may sound like more than the average person or the average family can do. It is not, especially when connected with the broader strength of the church. In fact, I am amazed at how mundane and ordinary the essence of our ministry here is. It is based on availability and openness. As Steve Morris, a friend and long-time inner-city minister, says, "Ministry at its core is simple. It involves following the initiative of Jesus as he connects us to people he wants to serve." Both Tina and the students in our household have done that by taking dessert to women in the neighborhood, watching their children, helping kids and teens with their homework, stopping by to talk or providing a quiet living room or back yard for some refuge. Service, interest and involvement communicate love.

Partnering with the Poor
But we've also communicated love by working alongside those in this neighborhood who are poor, in a specific pattern of partnership that

recognizes and maintains their dignity. Many Christians are adverse to serving the poor, for a variety of reasons. Some want the poor to have a certain image of goodness or nobility before they can feel good about serving them. Others don't like how awkward it feels to give charity. Others are afraid of being taken advantage of. But working in partnership with the poor to solve the problems cuts across all of those concerns. It does, however, require *involvement,* and living in such close proximity to the problems has provided the context for us to get involved.

For example, it is recognized that the Lowell Neighborhood physically looks bad. There are sixty-one condemned properties or empty lots on this one square mile of land. There is a lot of graffiti on buildings and walls. Neighbors generally agree that we can't just focus on the long-term problems of poverty and the breakdown of community without reference to the fact that the whole place needs a facelift. To address the physical deterioration of the neighborhood, college students in our ministry (InterVarsity Christian Fellowship) have been working with a coalition of people from the neighborhood and from other Christian agencies (Youth for Christ, Evangelicals for Social Action and World Impact) to bring change. Houses are being painted, alley lights installed; children are being read to; trash is being picked up; women are being given chances to know each other and vision is being built. In nearly all cases, it is a mix of people from the neighborhood and those of us who have chosen to live here more intentionally who are forming these partnerships to transform the area.

It's amazing how motivated and hopeful people become when they understand that this is not some new government program but simply a collection of people with a vested interest in making things better. Partnership says, "I've committed myself to work together toward real change, and I've put all my eggs in this basket. I'm not holding cab fare back to the suburbs in my back pocket in case it doesn't work. I'm in this with you."

It is this kind of partnership with the poor that will change the face of the city. At its core it is simple, something we all have the tools for. Living it out can be complex, just like everything else in life where people are involved. But my family and I wouldn't still be here if it took more than a basic foundation of love or more than a mustard seed's worth of faith. We've learned that those in this neighborhood who are poor are not looking for us to come in with "the answers." If we were to announce that we had the answers, we would destroy the trust we have been working to establish. They are tired of community organizers doing studies and announcing programs. What they want is someone to join them—really join them—in the day-to-day work required to transform this area into something we can be proud of. As Jodie says, "We need to be 'Jesus with skin,' right there, real, alongside, something they can feel, see, touch and hold."

Living here has created an environment where neighbor-love actually means something in our lives. It has done that not only by giving us plenty of chances to practice it but also by putting us so close to the problems that we can't ignore them anymore. It has made me realize that my lack of awareness of the needs of the city was very convenient and comfortable.

Seeing Clearly, Loving Intently

Once we had worked through the myths and stereotypes surrounding the city, we were ready to really see what has been happening there. And once we were able to see what was happening, we became more inclined to enter relationships with people who were vastly different from us. The very act of involvement created love of neighbor. Love of neighbor led to the ability to identify not only the needs of the neighborhood but also the resources that already existed there. And once this happened, we were ready to treat our neighbors as partners in the healing of the neighborhood. It's the kingdom of God at work. Christianity is not so much an idea to be explored as a power to be released. When it is, its nature is to transform.

That power has been released, and it is transforming the Sargosa family. I mentioned our growing partnership with people and agencies focused on the healing of our neighborhood. During one summer our students worked with Evangelicals for Social Action to identify houses in the neighborhood that needed special attention. Painting one particular house opened the door to long-term relationships that will affect this area for some time. Children from the neighborhood helped paint the house—and a process was begun which is breeding partnerships of all kinds.

The house belongs to Mrs. Sargosa. It's just a block from our home. She lives there with four of her six children. Her husband left her two years ago for another woman. She speaks little English. Her two oldest boys were involved in gangs and are now in prison, the oldest one for murdering the ice cream man, a crime that horrified the entire community. Her two daughters are in intermediate and high school and her two youngest sons in elementary school. They are children already treading the margins of society, ready to follow in the footsteps of their older brothers.

During the painting, one of our students discovered that Mrs. Sargosa's older daughter, Grace, was failing her high-school civics class. She was the first in her family to get close to finishing high school. But if she did not achieve a B on the final exam, she would not graduate. Grace had struggled to stay in school and was very close to finishing, but her failing grade made being the first graduate in her family seem a million miles away.

Instead of painting, Colleen decided to tutor Grace. She spent several days helping her study (and answering tons of questions about Jesus too). Then Grace took the final exam. She aced the test and graduated from high school. I learned two months later that Grace was registered for entrance into the city college.

But it doesn't end here. Other agencies found out that the heating in the house was not working and the floors were rotten. The city was enlisted for repairs, using revitalization money. Mrs. Sargosa's children were recruited by a Youth for Christ staffworker to go to a Joy of Jesus summer camp. Young boys are taken out of the city for the summer and given a taste of another life, then assigned a mentor—a Christian older brother—when they return.

Where it seemed a foregone conclusion that these boys would follow in the footsteps of their older brothers, they now have role models who are showing them alternatives and introducing them to the Savior. One of these boys, Juan, comes regularly to our house to eat with us and watches an occasional basketball game on TV with us. The youngest daughter asked Christ to be her Lord this year and is growing. Their lives will be different, and so will the neighborhood because of it. Because the neighborhood will be different, and because we are part of the simple yet profound ways in which the Lord is working here, we will be different too.

Questions for Reflection or Discussion

1. How does the command "love thy neighbor" sound in today's individualistic climate, where even knowing your neighbor's name is unusual, and where we make our friendships primarily based on interests rather than proximity?

2. What barriers exist in your life that might prevent you from seeking a crosscultural friendship—or that might rule out living in a part of town where most people are ethnically different from you?

3. If "partnering with the poor" sounds intimidating, what one step might you or your group take to simply increase your contact or involvement with people who are poor?

5/What's Good for the Goose . . .

■

*Fathers and mothers have lost the idea
that the highest aspiration they
might have for their children is for them
to be wise—as priests, prophets or
philosophers are wise. Specialized
competence and success are all that they
can imagine.*

*The dreariness of the family's spiritual
landscape passes belief. It is as
monochrome and unrelated to those who
pass through it as are the barren steps
frequented by nomads who take
their mere subsistence and move on.*
—*ALLAN BLOOM IN* THE CLOSING OF
THE AMERICAN MIND

T HE QUESTIONS CAME AT US LIKE A HOT WIND AS WE PREPARED
to move. What about all the influences that our move to the Lowell
Neighborhood would unleash on the lives of our children? Shouldn't
responsible parents attempt to calculate the effect on their kids' lives?
And what about the opinion of the children? Shouldn't parents who
are considering making a move to the inner city involve their children
in the decision? Shouldn't they give them a real voice in the process?

Our boys were ten and seven as we were talking it through. Though
it felt risky, we decided to make them equal partners. It would have to
be a unanimous yes or it would be a no go. If they said yes, we wanted
it to be with as much advance information as possible.

They had all the concerns one would expect. "Will there be someone to play with?" "Will it be safe?" "Will we be able to play outside without you watching?" "What school will we go to?" Some questions we couldn't answer. Others we answered as completely and honestly as we could. We talked about what "safe" meant, in light of the myths and realities about the city, but also in light of the real presence of God in our lives. In the end, their questions were all asked, our prayers for guidance were all offered, and they came to the point where they wanted to go.

Joseph and Jameson didn't ask all the questions that could have been asked. We introduced other things we thought they should consider. But we tried not to dump the whole story on them all at once. We responded to the questions they did have and let others develop after we had made the decision. It was amazing to see the ways in which the tiny grasp they had of their parents' vision for the move developed into a full, kid-sized idea which they owned. We concluded that while part of their willingness came from the reasons we described to them for the move, another part of it came from an embryonic call which God was planting in *their* lives.

God was not just calling the dad in this family to go and drag his family along. It was a call for the whole family. If that was true, then we guessed God had an agenda for each of us once we got there. That was certainly true for Tina, and I've asked her to share her thoughts here.

And Now a Word from the Mom

My first impressions of life here in Lowell centered around all the things that were *different* from my world: people of all kinds and colors, dirty streets, lots of graffiti, and a busier atmosphere because of the mixture of businesses and homes on our street. There was also lots of foot traffic; people always seemed to be walking everywhere. These weren't things I was afraid of, but they were initially intimidating. Because of the greater number of people on foot, using the bus or "hanging out" on porches, I was more aware of who was around me and what they were doing.

At first I would not pull into the alley at night to put the car away;

I would park on the street and have Randy put it away later. Now I pull right into the alley day or night, though I am cautious. The first sounds of gunfire made my heart jump, and the sound of loud conversations on the street late at night was unnerving. It was also maddening. We have called 911 on occasion, when the gunfire was close to the house. But in spite of these things, I found that safety precautions here were pretty much the same as in our old, "safe" neighborhood.

Now, having lived here for several years, I drive back here from working or visiting in the north part of town and it truly feels like coming "home." Having friends and neighbors here has made all the difference. The families whom we joined here and the others who moved here with us have become partners and friends to us. My support base comes from the wives of these families. We meet weekly to share, pray and debrief the week. There are other women I have met in the neighborhood through the very average circumstances of being neighbors. On Wednesday evenings my friend Glady and I host women from the neighborhood who come to my home for "ladies' night." Glady and I initially went door to door on a few of the streets to personally invite women; some came because of this contact, but others have come because they were brought by friends. It's an ethnically diverse group, and I have really enjoyed these new relationships. We do Bible study, play games, or sometimes just go out for coffee or to a special event.

The most frightening things about living here are the gang activity and the gunfire, but there is a sense among us that we are all in it together. The relationships I am forming give me a feeling of security and support.

The other great part of living here has been having college students live with us. There is always someone around (lights on, activity in the house), which helps with the safety issue. There is rarely a time when I'm here alone. In addition, these students help our children with their homework, watch them occasionally while I am on an errand, and provide instant friendship and companionship.

Initially we chose to keep our children at the Christian school they attended before our move, at least for a while. We didn't want to uproot their entire world all at once. But our intent is to ease them into schools in the neighborhood as they are ready. Every family's situation is different, and every child is different. We have friends in the neighborhood who moved in that direction immediately, and for them it seemed right.

This is my home, and for me home means family and extended family: friends and neighbors who know me and have been in my home, and a very supportive church family that worships just a mile from here. I also enjoy our Sunday evening family times within our household: we talk through our week, do Bible study concerning community lifestyle and resolve any problems that have arisen during the week.

Using our home in this way has meant making choices about how I keep my house—choices that were difficult for me at first. For example, because our living room hosts so many children in reading clubs, college students in Bible studies, women from the neighborhood (and sometimes it feels like the whole neighborhood itself), I've decided not to make it a place decorated with all the knickknacks and pretty things I would normally display. It's just not practical, and it might be construed by some as flaunting our wealth. But I've realized that I value having a living room full of people rather than things.

In the midst of all the changes—a new neighborhood, more people living in the house, the challenge of finding ways to be God's servant here—I need times of solitude, quiet getaways. So I have a desk next to our bed which is *my* space, where I go to be alone. Randy and the boys respect the closed door when I'm "retreating" at my desk.

I've had to work outside the home part time due to financial pressures, and more often than not the combination of work, family needs, household relationships and neighborhood ministry leaves me exhausted. We work hard as a family and as a married couple to get away once in a while to recover. We have both realized the need to find times for the four of us to create memories, not only here but away as well.

My life is different here from what I might have chosen were I left to myself. It began as Randy's vision. But it wasn't long before the move became my idea as well. Now that we are here, I wouldn't want anything else. This is good for me. The circumstances of our life here and of the neighborhood keep me from getting to the stage in my Christian life where I am numbed by being too comfortable. I'm very thankful to be here. Now back to Randy.

A Family Call

God calls families. It has been that way from the beginning. God called Abraham to leave Ur, but his entire family went with him. The covenant God made with Abraham clearly indicated that God intended to make Abraham a blessing to the people he would encounter (Gen 12:1-3). That would happen through his family. On a larger scale, God called Abraham's offspring, a family that grew to millions as the nation of Israel, to leave Egypt for a new land. There they were to live out the call to be a blessing.

In the New Testament, God is still calling whole families to respond to him. Jesus' family was called to relocate from Joseph's hometown to Bethlehem, then to Egypt, and finally to Nazareth. Whole families in the early life of the church came face to face with God and had to respond. Cornelius learned through an angel that he and his whole family would be saved (Acts 11:13-14). The Philippian jailer responded to Paul and Silas's miraculous escape with the decision to have his whole family baptized (Acts 16:29-34). Lydia's entire household was baptized in response to Paul's ministry in Philippi (Acts 16:15). God breaks through in the life of the family, and the gospel changes that family's direction forever. Not only does he call a family to faith together—sometimes he calls it to suffer together (Acts 8:3) and certainly to serve together (Acts 18:26).

We had guessed that God was calling us as a family to respond to him by moving to Lowell. After we moved, we realized early on that we had been called there not only to be agents of renewal *in* that fragmented and fractured neighborhood, but also for the work that God would do *through* that neighborhood in our lives.

Before the move, we had begun to feel that our lives were too comfortable, stunted even, by our cozy routines and calculated goals.

The question of whether we might be settling for mediocrity for ourselves and our boys plagued us. Like most parents, we had ideas about who we wanted our children to become. We could list values that we hoped they were catching, and we could identify areas of their lives that pleased us. But we also felt the powerlessness that so often terrorizes moms and dads these days. Even when we worked hard at instilling positive, biblical foundations in our children's lives, those seemed overwhelmed by the tide of destructive values that our culture kept effortlessly inculcating in them.

It was a wonderful surprise, then, after about a year in Lowell, when it began to dawn on us that we were seeing things develop in each family member that we had always prayed for but were at a loss to orchestrate. It was as if we as a family had unwittingly enrolled in a year-long class: Biblical Values 101. The city became our teacher, and, almost without thinking, we began to absorb its instruction. This was our primary call as a family: to sit at the feet of the city and live out the true meaning of the word *disciple.* We were called to be *learners.*

Urban Family Institute

Life in the Lowell Neighborhood is a raucous parade, weaving its way in and out of both the streets and the circumstances of this piece of land. With each pass it shapes us by calling assumptions into question, forcing decisions, confronting us with realities and providing opportunities that our suburban life never offered. It's the parade that, like a divinely orchestrated curriculum, has been silently, slowly and surely changing us. We may not come out with a diploma and a degree from this "urban family institute," but the growth is already apparent. What follows are just a few of the things we see happening in our lives.

Leadership and outreach. Parents struggle to help their children move beyond the egocentrism of infancy to acquire the ability to think of others, to act unselfishly and to live generously. We used to talk about these things, make the standard admonition to share toys, try to model an evangelistic lifestyle and so on. But we never felt very successful at producing in our kids the ability to take initiative in the lives of others or to reach out when they saw a need that they could meet.

One day, within just a few weeks of our move, I looked out the window and saw my boys leading a soccer clinic with some of the neighborhood kids. I hadn't asked them to do it. It was a warm summer morning, and they must have had ten children gathered around them in the open lot next to our house. Many of the kids spoke limited English or none at all, but they were dribbling the ball around cones, passing and stopping, scoring, laughing and running. When I came outside they were on their backs looking up at the sky. Sensing a teachable moment, we handed out "wordless gospel" bracelets to each child and told the story of the colors (gray for sin, red for Jesus' blood, clear for a clean heart, green for Christian growth, and gold for heaven). The children listened intently, and by the tenth child they all told the story back to us flawlessly. To top it off, Joseph, just eleven at the time, took off the new cross he had just bought with his own money and gave it to one of the children. He did it spontaneously and joyfully. Whenever he sees that child in the neighborhood he talks with her. All of this represents an unprecedented level of initiative on our boys' part—and in a new and strange environment.

Then there was the time I came out of my office into the living room one afternoon to find my sons putting on a mini Bible club for a handful of neighborhood kids. Some were so young or so limited in English that they couldn't understand, but they were having fun. Older children were clearly tracking. My guys were creating a game of memorizing their favorite Bible verse, John 3:16. "Are these *my* kids?" I laughed. Months later, those neighbor kids could still recite that verse.

And there have been smaller but still significant indications of growth. For example, one evening Jameson shocked us all by his prayer at the dinner table. It being his turn to pray, we all waited to hear the normal "thank you for this day . . . let this food nourish our bodies . . . help the 49ers win the Superbowl" kind of prayer that tends to be par for the course at nine years of age. Instead, on this occasion, we heard a heartfelt plea for God to work in the neighborhood, to change the lives of specific children whom he named, to help with the tutoring program and to protect our neighbors.

The language he used and the conceptual thinking he employed startled me. His vision for the reality of God at work surpassed that of many adults. Many rich and thankful thoughts filled my mind before I took my first bite of that meal. Since then, I have continued to notice that Jameson's prayers reflect both a childlike insight into the mind of God and a growing understanding of ministry.

It became clear to me that our environment had become a "switch" that was now electrifying in my boys a natural flow of leadership and sparking the desire to reach out which is planted by God in the hearts of those who know him. I realized that the *needs* of the Lowell Neighborhood, somehow clear and meaningful to their preadolescent minds, were coming together with the plentiful *opportunities* for ministry in the area. Service, initiative and outreach then were natural responses. When we talked about these values in the midst of the Lowell Neighborhood, they seemed more relevant and applicable. Leadership and outreach became less of a "should" and more of a natural course of action.

Our children are learning that families are more than just havens. And they are getting a message that there is something wrong if families become so self-focused that they are unable to see anything beyond their own intimacy as the goal of togetherness. Such a truncated vision of the purpose of family—valuing closeness but forgetting mission—is not only unsatisfying but dangerous for the soul. As James Burtshaell says, "The only home which is safe for anyone to be born into is the home that is ready to welcome someone who does not belong there by right of kinship, but belongs there in virtue of hospitality."[1] Our big house in the city is teaching us these things.

Reinforcing the right values. One of culture's most powerful messages to us today is that a quality life can be built around getting and consuming. Children are especially susceptible to this influence, and the thousands upon thousands of TV commercials that mesmerize and mentor them through their formative years wield a power which we are only now beginning to understand. Even as we attempt to limit television watching and mute the commercials, it is so frustrating to see how subtly and powerfully the message of acquisition gets into the minds and hearts of kids. The power of media in general and TV in particular to actually create culture (and not just mirror it) is hardly questioned anymore.

Allan Bloom states it bleakly when he says (even if with a touch of understandable hyperbole), "Parents can no longer control the atmosphere of the home and have even lost the will to do so. With great subtlety and energy, television enters not only the room, but also the tastes of old and young alike, appealing to the immediately pleasant and subverting whatever does not conform to it."[2]

In this kind of environment, how can our children acquire a life posture of valuing people over things, substance over image, character and purpose over entertainment? I'll spend more time in the next chapter describing how living in an intentional community with college students has taught us precious lessons about ourselves and about what it means to be the body of Christ. But here I want to focus on just one of the most substantial and lasting effects of the community on my family. It is the power and interest of the human story, when it is prominent in a family's dialogue, that keeps a family's focus on people rather than on the hamster wheel of acquisition. It's the force of the drama of everyday life that rightly steals the show and keeps us thinking about our purpose and direction so that we are not distracted by passions and thrills.

Much of our family's dialogue happens when the entire household is together before, during and after dinner. This was not always the case. Dinners in our old house were often silent breaks in the exhaustion of the schedule, refueling stations where we tried to connect with each other between mouthfuls of potato. But our expanded family here, which includes the students who live with us and their friends who drop by, makes dinner time a more formal experience of community—and makes the dialogue possible. It is here that the human story unfolds in all of its banality and glory, its mystery and humor. Dinners, and the interactions which often spill over into the kitchen or living room afterward, become exciting reviews of that day's script in the drama rather than perfunctory recitations of what we did today.

I am amazed at how few families these days even observe a stated dinner hour, let alone talk about things there that matter. I have often asked my college students to talk about what dinner time at their homes was like when they were growing up. Even for intact families it was revealing. Bloom's description of the American family is close to the mark when he says that "the family has, at best, a transitory togetherness. People sup together, play together, travel together, but they do not think together. Hardly any homes have any intellectual life whatsoever, let alone one that informs the vital interests of life."[3] I don't know whether it is truly that dismal. But from what I'm hearing and seeing in the students I work with, it's close.

As the dinner conversations in our household revolve around the latest happenings in the neighborhood, the things we are doing with people in our various forms of service here, and what people think or feel about it all, I watch my children listening. They take it all in. The power of story keeps them there. And we are finding that, rather than asking to go to the mall for a little worship—I mean shopping—after dinner, the children, adults and semiadults in the house would rather be together, rather be involved in each other's stories; they don't want to miss anything. They're catching a value we felt completely unskilled to give them. People are more exciting than things. Being together is more interesting than playing in isolation with the latest electronic toy.

Positive models: examples of faith. We always wanted our children to grow up around people who modeled a real faith, one with hands and feet. We wanted them to know the stories of those who attempted great things for God and expected great things of God. And since children grow to value and follow the voices and examples of people other than their parents, we wanted them exposed to Christians whose faith was vital and animated, who were really making a difference and feeling the difference in their own lives. We wanted them to get the message that this was what we were put together for as human beings. We were not designed to exist in a series of endless self-preoccupations. The life-breath for Christians is risking the sacrificial love and service that Jesus lived out. We wanted Joseph and Jameson to grow up believing that "service is the rent we pay for living."[4]

But beyond Bible readings, parental sermonettes and our own flawed examples, what was there in our lives that could provide a steady stream of persuasion toward a vital faith and a courageous servanthood?

College students are great for this. My children see them walking the streets of our neighborhood building friendships with children, teens and families who are vastly different from them. They hear students rejoicing in the progress of these relationships and agonizing over setbacks. They see students building outreach into their schedules and having to plan study and leisure time around ministry. They see them pursuing the appropriate training for their eventual vocations but doing ministry as they go. They hear the students praying for the neighborhood. Now my children's prayers echo their words and phrases. The college students who have joined our family are living examples of the truths and principles we as parents have tried to convey. And since my kids think students are cool, and my students think Jesus is cool, my kids think Jesus is cool. What an incredible gift our life here in Lowell is becoming to my family.

Negative models: a parade of dysfunctions. But students have brought more than their wonderful models of faith and outreach. They have brought all of the dysfunctions of their backgrounds and the inclination toward sin that characterizes the human condition. They have brought them to live at our house like silent, sinister, invisible roommates. When one considers the amount of energy required of parents just to work through our own negative influence on the lives of our kids, inviting others to bring theirs too seems almost irresponsible. But we have learned that God is using even this for the good of our family.

Every parent knows that kids think in pictures. Abstract concepts are difficult to grasp, requiring a sophistication that comes only in later years. The more concrete the concept, the easier to explain. We learned this playing games like charades. Words like *chair* or *book* or *lamp* were easy. They were objects, and one could point to them. But when we were assigned words that, instead of describing objects, conveyed concepts, like *poverty* or *cruelty* or *benevolence,* it became much more difficult to communicate by gestures. Pointing to things is always easier.

So it is with some of life's lessons as well. When things happen in the lives of our students that are the consequences of bad choices, our children have questions, and the circumstances become opportunities to teach them about life. These are complex things that might be hard for children to understand. But sometimes we don't need to do the teaching; the situation is clear enough to convey the lesson. All we have to do then is point, and our children understand. When one of our students would do near back-flips to avoid conflict, our boys noticed, and we talked about it. When another student lived with a massive fear of making mistakes, our boys noticed, and we talked about it. When a student didn't follow through on commitments or dropped the ball on things, our boys noticed, and we talked about it. And when our own sin and dysfunctionalities as parents arose, others in the house noticed, and *everyone* talked about it!

Nothing is lost in the economy of God. Both good and bad become contexts in which to learn. The community living in our big house in the city is a vast and rich source of these lessons.

Confrontation and conflict. No one likes confrontation. For those few people who do like it, it often seems that no one likes *them!* I've noticed that Christians, especially, tend to avoid even constructive confrontation. We value niceness and tolerance so highly that we are willing to sacrifice relationship, which is what happens when conflict is overlooked. But not dealing with the issues and interactions that divide us, even in the name of niceness, is destructive and will never allow reconciliation to take place. In contrast, those who face each other to deal with their differences come out stronger.

I'll never forget the time one of the students living with us asked me if he could speak to my son Joseph, who was about eleven years old at the time. He wanted me there too. I could tell as we sat down that something was wrong, and it soon became clear that some difficult business was at hand.

The student was concerned about his relationship with Joseph: he felt there had been occasions where he and Joseph weren't treating each other as well as they could. The confrontation came as a surprise to my son, though he acknowledged there was a problem.

Not everyone has experience with what children can handle at the different stages of their growth or how to approach them with a problem. And though he didn't intend it, this student stated the problem—though accurately—in what I felt were overly stark terms. As I observed the conversation before me, I could tell that Joseph wasn't ready for this, and I was not surprised when he began to cry. At first I felt resentment. I wondered if the student couldn't have been a little gentler, a little more aware of the fact that he was speaking to an eleven-year-old and not a peer. But I just put my arm around my son and helped him share his perspective on the whole thing. Having told each other what the problem was, they talked about solutions and then prayed together.

I figured that after such a difficult experience it would be impossible for Joseph to have much of a relationship with this student. But in the weeks and months to come, I was amazed to see a new strength in their friendship. Because the confrontation had happened, even though it happened a bit more severely than I would have liked, it gave them the opportunity to work through their differences to a real reconciliation.

Even if the process of dealing with differences is messy, if both parties are really interested in reconciliation and are willing to do the work of pursuing it, it is still worth the emotional price tag that often accompanies it. Living in community in the city has put a sort of "holy pressure" on our lives to deal with these things.

That confrontation was a valuable lesson, both for my son and for me. As other conflicts have come to the surface, as they will in community, we are becoming more inclined to do the hard work of facing them and using them for good.

Courage. The great American aviator Amelia Earhart said, "Courage is the price that Life exacts for granting peace. . . . The soul that knows it not, knows no release from little things."[5] Facing the things that cause fear in our lives often brings freedom. Whether it is standing in front of an audience to which one is required to speak or driving down a certain street that has always caused uneasiness, actually doing it a few times can bring liberation from long-held anxieties.

Some of the "little things" that inject fear in our lives aren't so little. Our experience in Lowell has provided many opportunities to do things that routinely cause fear and anxiety. We walk streets where we are the only white people. (Our culture has taught us to fear this.) We relate with people who to us look physically threatening. (Our culture has taught us to judge by external measures.) We live in the midst of graffiti, boarded-up houses and dirty streets. (Our culture has taught us to stereotype and then fear what we don't understand.) The intimidation factor is present in some way each day, at levels ranging from infinitesimal to more serious.

But just dealing with these things on a routine basis has helped us understand ourselves and our environment, and fear is no longer controlling our choices. The resulting benefit is peace—peace in the midst of circumstances which, to the external eye, look anything but peaceful. We are finding that what Moses counseled is true for those who would make the Lord their refuge: "You will not fear the terror of night, nor the arrow that flies by day, nor the pestilence that stalks in the darkness. . . . A thousand may fall at your side, ten thousand at your right hand, but it will not come near you" (Ps 91:5-7). We have come to love and appreciate the neighborhood and the cultures represented here.

A Family Adventure
The American family today is in great need of adventure, and I don't mean more trips to Disneyland. Our vision of life is so small that we are instantly dissatisfied when we attain it. We are in need of an overarching purpose for the family—a purpose bigger than the family itself. Moving to the Lowell Neighborhood has been the most focusing experience of my family's life. First it scrambled our values, and then it created a wonderful new center.

The city has been an able teacher in leadership and outreach, a skilled provider of positive and negative role models, a jarring tutor in conflict resolution and a deliberate trainer in courage. There have been countless other areas of growth for us all. God has been faithful to lead the whole family, and not just the dad, into an exciting journey which is helping us all to mature in Christ. What I see happening in our family gives me hope that the powerful and pervasive cultural pressures that are exerted on a family—that try to twist and conform it to an impotent shallowness—cannot compete with the adventure that God is leading us through. The things God is producing in our lives are well worth the risks of the environment.

Questions for Reflection or Discussion

1. How are things like courage, leadership, an alive faith, the ability to confront, models of healthy relationships and so on developed in children?

2. In what ways might the lifestyle adjustments that God may be asking of his people actually bring greater joy and contentment than we expect?

3. What criteria can you use to discern God's call on the life of your family?

6/Like Working a Loom

■

Weave, weave, weave me the sunshine out
of the fallin' rain;
Weave me the hope of a new tomorrow,
fill my cup again . . .
—PETER, PAUL & MARY

It is clear that we are witnessing the
unraveling of America. Short
of a profound change of national
direction, this unraveling will continue,
and become more brutal.
—JIM WALLIS IN THE SOUL OF POLITICS

"Tapestry" is a very good way to de-
scribe a community.
—BOB LUPTON IN THEIRS IS THE KINGDOM

JUST A YEAR AFTER I HAD COMMITTED MY LIFE TO CHRIST, I leapt at the chance to go with my church on a tour of the Holy Land. The places mentioned in the Bible, most often the cities, began to jump off the page as we "walked where Jesus walked." During our time in Jerusalem we were free to investigate the tangled streets of the old city, which were crowded with vendors and various others ready to capitalize on the regular flow of pilgrims. But the warm beauty of the amber stones of Jerusalem could not in any way be diminished by the commercialism, and I loved to weave my way in and out of the low walls and alleys, pushing past the polished in search of that which was genuine.

On one occasion, I came upon a small shop which sold fabrics and woven tapestries. I was looking for something that symbolized my time in the city. A weaving or wall hanging seemed perfect. But budget concerns pressed me to settle instead on a machine-made tapestry of deer looking out from a forest. I later guessed that it had been made in Hong Kong. I was hoping for a piece of handwork someone had labored over, carefully choosing threads and patterns, perhaps making mistakes and fixing them—something which, in the end, they were even reluctant to part with. What I ended up with was far less costly—and far less valued. After quickly tiring of it back home, I eventually gave it to a thrift store.

Weaving an Urban Tapestry

In *Theirs Is the Kingdom,* Bob Lupton pictures neighborhoods as intricate weavings. "Tapestry is a very good way to describe a community, especially an urban community. Individual fibers are spun into unique threads and woven into a colorful collage of real life. The warp and woof of relationships give it strength. The continuity of its boundaries holds it together."[1]

Lupton has got it right for urban communities, and this is a good description of Lowell. But I want to build on his metaphor a bit and talk about the loom itself, the apparatus that does the weaving. It's an awkward-looking machine, yet beautiful in its ability to connect simple fibers into complex patterns of texture and color.

Those who would seek to turn a neighborhood around are taking turns at operating a giant loom. In attempting the revitalization of a neglected neighborhood, or should we say those neighborhoods which, because of crime, unemployment, drugs and the breakup of the family, have been unraveling for generations, we are learning that the weavers—those who operate the loom—must combine two essential strands of fiber. These are the ministries of *compassion* and *development.* We need to combine *betterment programs* and *structural change.*

Helping Out and Helping Up

Reweaving the frayed fabric of a neighborhood takes the ability to see the existing needs from both a short-term and a long-term perspective. When we moved into Lowell, some of the needs were instantly obvious. Kids had nothing to do after school, were behind in their education and often came from lousy and even dangerous home situations. Graffiti and boarded-up homes created an intimidating environment. So we started doing tutorial programs and organizing paint crews. We began building relationships, praying for our neighbors and orchestrating ways for neighbors to meet one another.

All of these steps have been important, even foundational for our ministry. Any neighborhood revitalization plan that is not built on this strategy of direct person-to-person help has little hope of being any more effective than the failed urban policies put forward by the federal government over the last several decades. Because real change happens when real people change, attempts to bring transformation without a renewal of the spirit of the people end up being merely cosmetic.

Lisa, a young woman from our neighborhood, is a good illustration of that principle. The child of a violent, alcoholic father, Lisa lived in twenty-two foster homes before she reached adulthood. She had a child, whom she put up for adoption. She had lived a marginal existence in codependent relationships in the poorest neighborhood in the city ever since.

Lisa had come occasionally to a gathering of neighborhood women which Tina and our friend Glady organized in our home. Women shared their lives, did crafts and Bible studies, took outings and became friends there. But Lisa's situation continued to deteriorate when her father and brother, who lived nearby, threatened her life. She even feared going on her paper route in the mornings, her only source of income.

One evening, unable to take the burden of her life any longer, she left her house determined to bring it all to an end. As she walked the streets of Lowell looking for a way to kill herself, she remembered that women came to our house on Wednesdays to share and pray. It was Wednesday. That night Lisa found women who cared about her, who lived in the neighborhood and were available right then to listen to her troubles. She has been coming to the group regularly, has shared her story in increasing detail and now has friends who will listen. An agency couldn't have helped Lisa at that moment, even if she had known how to get to the right one. Social workers were unavailable and church offices were closed in the evening. She didn't need to be referred; she needed someone right there, right then.

But Lisa's situation also illustrates a corresponding principle that is crucial in our attempts at revitalizing Lowell. Unless there is a growing sense of partnership between people and agencies in coordinating the reweaving process, the collective unraveling of individual lives in the neighborhood will continue to undo the whole cloth. Until the issues that contribute to the unraveling are dealt with at a very basic and long-term level, our efforts at showing compassion will end up ignoring the wider problem and will perpetuate the shortsighted strategy of the church historically: it has majored in charity rather than real transformation.

The Bible's approach to this issue is much more radical than tutoring programs and individual outreach, though a biblical process of renewal would include things like that. The Bible is interested in justice applied in a community at all levels.

Jubilee!

Justice at all levels. That is what was behind the part of the Law known as the jubilee. Leviticus 25 outlines God's intention that all land return to its original owner every fifty years, so the rich would not acquire all the land and squeeze out the poor.

When someone fell into debt, their land and even their children were at risk of being used to satisfy the debt. All sorts of things led to debt: death of the father in the family, a poor harvest, physical limitations and so on. Jubilee was God's way of leveling the playing field before whole sectors of society were marginalized. Ron Sider reminds us that the theological principle behind this startling command was that God was the owner of all the land in the first place, and we are just stewards of it.[2]

"The land must not be sold permanently, because the land is mine and you are but aliens and my tenants" (Lev 25:23). But the jubilee wasn't just a governmental mandate. It recognized that the structure of the law would simply support what the poor would be able to accomplish with the return of their land. "The jubilee principle also provides for self-help and self-development. With his land returned, the poor person could again earn his own living. The biblical concept of jubilee underlines the importance of institutionalized mechanisms and structures that promote justice."[3]

Similar to the year of jubilee was the corresponding concept of the sabbatical year. Every seventh year slaves were to be freed, debts on loans were to be canceled, the land was to be given rest from cultivated harvests and the poor could glean from what grew naturally.

But I'm not advocating the flat and static application of either the jubilee or the sabbatical-year laws in our culture. Rather, it is the spirit of the jubilee and sabbatical year and the comprehensive nature of the justice they proposed—a justice that affected the whole community—which we should seek to mimic. We should be concerned that some in our community need food and clothing. But our concern must not address only these needs. It must extend to their housing situations, their need for job training, the education of their children, the safety of the streets, the health of their souls and their hope for the future.

Perhaps the most recognized symbol of the pride of our country, outside the flag itself, is the Liberty Bell, which hangs in Philadelphia. It symbolically rings out the words "Proclaim liberty throughout the land." Ron Sider reminds us that those words come from the biblical passage on jubilee (Lev 25:10).[4] Christians can recapture the sense of commitment that our country's founders had to the broad application of the spirit of jubilee in our early history. But he challenges, "Do Christians have the courage to demand and implement the structural changes needed to make that ancient inscription a contemporary reality?"[5]

It is inherent in the nature of the jubilee principle that it works only if it is applied consistently from several sides at once. This is true whether we are attempting to apply it in an individual's life or in the reweaving of a whole neighborhood. Like the sewing circles of the

Appalachian mountains, where women would bring their favorite swatches of fabric and sit in a circle to sew them together into a quilt, we must approach the goal of community revitalization from many sides at once.

Because there is no evidence that Israel ever even attempted to implement the jubilee, we can only surmise that it seemed as radical and all-encompassing, as naive and even dangerous to them as it seems to us. Yet in the Lowell Neighborhood we are attempting to bring some of the spirit of jubilee to bear. Part of that involves bringing to the circle the expertise of each individual and organization that will link their lives and resources to the renewal of Lowell. We will not consider *only* the need for spiritual renewal or *only* the need for streetlights. We will not major in either evangelism *alone* or social action *alone*. We will each bring what we can, but we must all bring to the table something that addresses the whole picture. And if there is a gap around the table, someone else must be invited to become part of a long-term solution.

This is what happened when some of us met Betty. A single mom, Betty had been living with her two children in a motel in the downtown area which was a notorious center for drugs, prostitution and the homeless mentally ill. The residents are charged twice what it would cost them for decent housing in an apartment, but few of them can save up for the first and last month's rent and the security deposit that is so often required. So they pay a premium price for a room so small that when you open the door it hits the bed. Large families squeeze in there. Betty had come from a background that included drug abuse, and all of her friends were either locked into that lifestyle or touched in some way by it. The cockroaches, filth, constant noise and chaotic environment of the Vargas Motel made life awful, but she felt she had few options.

A few years earlier, World Impact, an inner-city ministry that works with children and families in impoverished areas, decided they wanted to focus on the children living in the Vargas Motel. They staffed their Bible club program with college students from InterVarsity Christian Fellowship. This matured into a wonderful partnership that benefited both organizations. World Impact got a steady stream of motivated staff, and InterVarsity got a learning posture that took students out of their safe, insulated environment on campus into the real world. This Bible club was where we met Betty and her kids.

When the residents were eventually asked to leave the decaying motel, Project Home Again, another agency in our coalition, stepped in and helped Betty find a house she could afford. As it happens, ESA's Love Thy Neighbor Project had just painted that house as part of their revitalization efforts on that street. Our InterVarsity college students helped her move and maintained relationships with her children. A representative from Youth for Christ visited her and got her kids involved in a youth club.

In this past year alone, she has made a recommitment to Christ, joined a church in the Lowell Neighborhood (both attending and volunteering) and severed relationships with her old drug crowd. She is helping out at the local school and has joined the Entrepreneurial Training Center, a program run by Evangelicals for Social Action/Love Inc. and designed to help low-income women begin their own businesses and get off welfare.

A quick count of the agencies or ministries I highlighted reveals at least six parties around the table partnering with Betty for the reweaving of the fabric of her life. Betty is being helped—and so is everyone who is touched by her positive influence in the neighborhood.

The Loom: Agencies and Neighbors Linking Up
Betty's experience is an example of an individual family benefiting from interagency cooperation. But it is also symbolic of how the whole Lowell Neighborhood will be turned around. We are attempting to use that strategy for more than cooperative attempts at compassion and the betterment of individual situations. We are attempting a network of Christian agencies that will not only cooperate but actually link their purposes to addressing the factors in Lowell that act as snags to the existing yarn of the community.

Groups as diverse as Youth for Christ (a ministry to high-school students), Evangelicals for Social Action/Love Inc. (a network of church volunteers addressing various social needs), World Impact (an inner-city agency focusing on ministry to children and families through Bible clubs and church planting), InterVarsity Christian Fellowship (a ministry to college students), a local church, a retreat center and other groups have been blurring organizational lines in an attempt to bring lasting change. We are a coalition, but we are acting like a corporation in that we are sharing resources, doing joint fundraising and trying to channel some of the resources of our organizations to the neighborhood. Some of the heads of these agencies have moved into the neighborhood.

Our meetings are given to outlining strategies to meet needs: painting houses, forming a kids' club, planting a church or pioneering a tutoring program. But we are also attempting to deal with the lack of streetlights and speed bumps, the city's shortsighted housing plan, the need for curbs and gutters, graffiti abatement and street sweeping. This comprehensive approach weaves together the indigenous and colorful fibers of neighborhood residents with imported fibers that strengthen what is there.

This process hasn't been easy. The objectives of each organization have to remain in view but somehow also take a back seat if we are to make a difference. And building a philosophy of community development that combines the very different fibers of *betterment programs* and *community development* is an arduous process.

We have also struggled to understand the role of community residents themselves in the process of reweaving. They are both thread and loom. If we merely channel outside resources to "fix" the problems of the neighborhood, things will deteriorate again. Yet if we develop the indigenous materials of the neighborhood (natural leaders, for example) without regard for the spiritual dimensions of community development which the coalition of ministries fosters, then it means mere self-interest drives the process of revitalization. This will result only in the poor being driven from the neighborhood and a few developers making money. That kind of "revitalization" is fairly easy, makes great headlines, then deteriorates soon after the camera lights fade.

Limitations of the Loom

The loom is the mechanism that unites the threads of *compassionate outreach* and *structural change* in the neighborhood. What we need are Christians who will commit their lives to learning how to weave.

But the loom has limitations. In our case it was made up initially of middle-class, mostly white, educated evangelicals who, along with their ministries and families, unconsciously brought their worldview to the 'hood. That worldview assumed things about "community" which were shaped in very homogeneous environments and were not always relevant to the needs that existed here.

For example, one project we completed was the installation of new lights on one of the streets. It seemed like a good idea. But we never really asked what the main priorities of the people on that street were, and we did damage to the sense of partnership we had wanted to establish. It took some time to rebuild the trust. As we have built friendships with people already here, we are beginning to understand that they already have a very good sense of what the needs of the neighborhood are. On one street, we pulled way back with the initiative we were taking and instead worked on developing these relationships. Our cooperative approach now includes the cooperation of those already here, and we are learning to recognize our limitations.

Weavers' Guild

Without this cooperative approach, which focuses on both *individual* outreach and *community* development, we would not have moved here. The task would have seemed overwhelming and foolish. It was the network of families who were willing to move to Lowell and to attempt something new together which drew us here.

Now there are five families who, over the last five years, have chosen to relocate into Lowell. We meet monthly for a potluck to support one another and to stay connected, and some meet weekly to pray. This fellowship often includes other residents and nonresidents who care about the neighborhood. The process of cooperation is built on the foundation of commitment toward one another as persons, not as "major players in the revitalization of the neighborhood." We are people first, with life situations that change, and we often suffer from the inherent confusion which changing circumstances, not to mention the neighborhood itself, can engender.

It has been so helpful to have someone right here to call when stuff happens. One evening, as Tina and I were standing in the kitchen, we heard a series of gunshots come from a house nearby. We knew the house. Fanny had lived there for fifteen years, even after her husband moved out. She had had a series of lovers move in and out, and sometimes late at night we could hear her bloodcurdling scream. Her eleven-year-old daughter would mimic the scream for days afterward. Her son would be in and out of the place, wearing gang-banger clothes. She had been cordial to us but distant and unresponsive to our invitations.

As I ran out to see what had happened, Fanny was going to her car and yelling for some unknown person to get out of the house. There was a commotion inside. I yelled to Fanny, "Are you all right? What's happening?" She rolled her eyes and didn't answer. I was torn between going over there and calling the police. I called the police. Before they came, someone left the house with a bandage on his head. When the police arrived, I saw them talking to Fanny and heard her denying that anything had happened. They drove away without going inside, and I was left wondering what to do.

I called my friend Steve. He and his family had moved to Lowell long before we had. I wanted to know what my relationship with Fanny should be at this point and how to repair whatever damage had been done by my calling the police. He helped me formulate a response to her—one that communicated both my concern for her and a firm message that this kind of stuff would not go unnoticed and unreported in the neighborhood. We prayed, and within the hour I was able to talk with Fanny. I communicated both messages and also offered to pray for her or listen to her when problems arose. It became an opportunity to be a neighbor to her, even if an unwelcome neighbor.

Fanny remained unresponsive and less than honest about what had happened. But I was more of a neighbor to her than I would have been had I not called Steve to work it through. Together we wove a response to this snag, and the fabric of that corner of the neighborhood was held together a bit better than it would have been.

Those of us who have moved into this neighborhood and those who were here before us, trying to make a difference, have become a weavers' guild of sorts. We have knit ourselves together with cords of love to hold each other accountable, to create strategies and to design patterns of response to what we see happening around us. Mostly, we just encourage each other to stay at the loom.

Becoming Part of the Loom

A growing movement of God's people is personally addressing the unraveling of America's inner city and listening intently to God's call to reverse the decades-old trend toward abandoning it. Indeed, it was that trend which created the stubborn and entrenched cycles of poverty that characterize so many inner-city neighborhoods today. As Bob Lupton notes, the major contributor to this cycle is the "withdrawal of the middle class and the persistent hemorrhage of indigenous leadership."[6]

Individuals that "make it" tend to leave the urban neighborhood. That contributes to its further decline. But now some are staying, and some are coming back. It has been called the "relocation" movement, and a new word—*reneighboring*—has been coined to describe the core element of the strategy. God's people are returning to love the neighbors they once chose to abandon in their flight from the city. It is God's people—plain, middle-class folk—making the "return flight."[7]

But this is not a new strategy. As we read in the Old Testament, Nehemiah employed it thousands of years ago. When he learned that the city of Jerusalem was in ruins as a result of a Babylonian victory and a forced exile that drained the city's most promising youth and leadership, he was personally distressed and resolved to make the return flight (Neh 1).

We learn that the good hand of his God was on him as he asked the king for passage and permission to rebuild the wall of the city (chapter 2). The next several chapters tell how God used Nehemiah to work the miracle of a rebuilt wall as well as a rebuilt national identity for the discouraged, hassled, poverty-stricken remnant who lived in the rubble.

But building a wall was only the beginning of the challenge. In chapter seven, we learn that "the city was large and spacious, but there were few people in it, and the houses had not yet been rebuilt" (v. 4). The remnant were living in the villages surrounding the city; no one wanted to live in the unsecured ruins, even if they could reconstruct the housing situation. But chapter eleven reveals that a strategy of relocation was at the very core of Nehemiah's plan for remaking the city and restoring Israel's pride. It was a strategy based on leadership by example.

"Now the leaders of the people settled in Jerusalem" (11:1). They knew they had to start the movement themselves. When that happened, the people of God, caught up in the amazing work into which the hand of God had led them, committed their most precious resource to the rebuilding of the city. They took one out of ten of their sons and daughters and commissioned them to go and repopulate the city. They uprooted families, workers, new arrivals and the remnant poor and blessed them (11:1-2) with the call to rebuild the infrastructure of the city.

A quick look at the kind of people they sent is revealing. They sent craftsmen who could work on the temple (11:16) and singers to serve there (11:22-23), both groups helping to reweave the worship life of the nation, which had unraveled. They sent officials to govern the revitalization efforts of specific governmental districts (11:9). They commissioned a police force to guard the fragile security of the new neighborhoods (11:19). They sent a seasoned diplomat to ensure the welfare of the people (11:24). The economy was agriculturally based, but the renewal of employment and housing in the city undoubtedly helped to reestablish stability there.

What's impressive about all of this is how intentional and comprehensive this plan was. Nothing less would be effective, especially in light of the opposition they were getting all along. Sanballat and Tobiah, long-time residents and regional leaders, were not happy with the progress. Sensing a threat to their power, they opposed the plan. They had a vested interest in keeping Judah a depressed area, and they attempted on several occasions to sabotage the process. Like many industries today that ostensibly have risen to "serve" the community of the poor, they are likely to profit most if the poor stay as they are.

Were these folks who moved back into Jerusalem's city center missionary types? Were they part of that daredevil class of Yahweh followers who would do anything in his name? Were they the Mother Teresas of their day? No! They were average people who committed themselves to one another in a very real demonstration of community. They all had to pitch in or else this vast rebuilding project would flop. They were not hoping that someone else would do it. They would link their very lives to the reweaving of their community. Even if one might argue that since Israel was a theocracy and not a democracy, its citizens were more on task with God's agenda for the city, that does not excuse God's people today. Yet they were more focused in their obedience than the modern church seems to be.

The church can no longer ignore what is happening in our cities, or hide in the diminishing safety of our suburbs, or simply hope for a new social policy that will adequately address the disintegration. The answer, both to the growing fragmentation of the city and to our growing fear of the "urban wasteland" as it is characterized in our culture, is a recapturing of our courage, our sense of community and our commitment to the common good.

Bob Lupton reminds us that "withdrawal to places of privilege with no concern for those we have left behind is the American dream devoid of a social conscience."[8] That dream cannot be ultimately satisfying, especially for the Christian, as it is built on the very principle of loving oneself over one's neighbor—the opposite of what Jesus said was to be our highest guiding principle as believers.

Living that way will dig us deeper into the pit in which we have already become trapped. Again, to quote Lupton: "Abandoned neighborhoods, schools from which the children of achievers have been withdrawn, spiritual battlegrounds where evil triumphs while the strong retreat—this is the twentieth-century city, the bitter fruit of a

Christianity devoid of the essential doctrine of community." And he throws down the gauntlet before the church as he contends, "Perhaps in this urbanizing and suburbanizing era in history we need to create a new mission emphasis in the church—a Holy Order of Neighbors— to reestablish visible, living models of how God intended communities to work."[9]

Here Comes the City!

Even with the model of Nehemiah relocating to reinhabit the city, and even with Lupton's prophetic call to the creation of a "Holy Order of Neighbors," the most common reaction by the church today is this question: "Are you saying that all Christians should move to the city and become urban missionaries?"

This concern is becoming more and more irrelevant. The bare fact is, over the long run it will become less necessary for Christians to ask the question "Is God calling me [us] to take the 'return flight' to the city?" The city isn't waiting for us to come. It is expanding like "the blob that ate Chicago." *The city is moving to us,* and at an amazing rate. The word *megalopolis*[10] has been employed in the last decade to describe the effect achieved when towns once separated by country- side expand to the extent that their borders touch, creating in effect a huge new city.

For example, no one who refers to "Los Angeles" means just the city called Los Angeles. We mean all the surrounding communities and counties, the freeways, the fast-paced life and all the urban images that come across the TV screen at us, stretching from Anaheim's Disneyland to Pasadena's Rose Bowl. That's what we mean by Los Angeles.

"Today, the number of people living in cities outnumbers the entire population of the world 150 years ago."[11] By the year 2000 more than half of the world's population will live in urban centers.[12] All of this means that the children of the baby boomers, the so-called Generation X and the newly christened "millennial" generation will grow up and have their children in decidedly urban surroundings. Those who have purchased homes in the suburbs, hoping to avoid the problems of the central city, will find those problems tracking them down, penetrating even the most privileged and gated communities as they are swallowed by urban sprawl. And since many local governments make way for new developments at the edges of city boundaries without addressing the decay that often characterizes city centers, the end result is no more than a naive hope of building a "new city" while ignoring the cancer in its feet.[13]

To Stay or to Go?

Even if it is a minority of Christians in the short run who ask about God's call to the city, eventually Christians who find their neighborhoods changing will have to ask, *Do I go or do I stay?* Staying means linking their lives to the renewal of the city. To go, to seek escape, means to let the cancer run free. For both the human body and the anatomy of the city, that strategy merely ends in an agonizing death.

Another question is of a more personal nature. People ask, "How can you throw your money away by buying a house in a depressed area? Must relocation carry such a high personal price tag?"

We did give thought to this. It was hard not to. Before I had given my life to Christ and returned to college, I had sold real estate for a short while. I knew the "risk" we were taking. But our families and friends were very concerned about it. They saw us buying in the poorest and most crime-ridden community in Fresno. Everything about the decision seemed wrong from the standpoint of conventional financial wisdom. The house itself would require lots of repair and maintenance. If the area were ever to turn around and homes become valuable here again, it probably wouldn't be in the near future.

What helped most (besides the obvious chance this gave us to store up treasures in heaven rather than on earth) was the thought that we were gaining a security of a different kind. I was always taught that you "trade up." Purchase to your limit, wait a while, then purchase up again. Your net worth goes up, and you are more and more secure.

Instead, we have chosen a "security in numbers" approach to life. Because our home is in a poor neighborhood, we got twice the house for half of what it would cost in a more affluent part of town. Because it is so large, we have students living with us, people who have become part of our family. They help share the cost of life here by helping to pay the mortgage, sharing food costs, watching our children when we are away. Life is very expensive here, but we feel every bit as secure financially as we did in the suburbs. The house may or may not appreciate. We may not even get out what we put in. But we will have gained.

In addition, we are following good tradition. During the period just before the capture of Jerusalem by Babylon, God told Jeremiah to buy a piece of land (Jer 32). Jeremiah's cousin wanted to get rid of it, since he could see that Babylon was soon to own title anyway, and he shamelessly hit up his cousin Jeremiah, who was in jail at the time, to buy it. It made no sense. The deed would be worthless. But God had something more powerful in mind. This purchase would say to all the people watching, "One day this land will be valuable again. God will redeem it when he returns us to the land." It was to be a powerful statement of hope, in spite of how it looked. It was not a bad invest-ment. It was an investment with a long-range payoff but with imme-diate significance. That's what our move is all about.

Though this is the hardest thing we've ever done, we feel more connection to God's agenda in this world than ever before. Even in the midst of the difficulties which are all part of the deal, we are experiencing the benefits of linking our lives to God's purposes. We are experiencing real community—the connecting of our lives to others who are engaged in something larger than their own needs or issues. We are walking in the midst of biblical models and promises and finding them to be true. And we are feeling the delight of God, who makes "well-watered gardens" of those who spend themselves on behalf of the poor (Is 58:10-11).

Questions and objections are welcome. Sometimes they come from others; sometimes they arise from our own hearts as we seek to understand and obey the heart of God. With regard to the questions that plagued my mind as I struggled with our call to relocate, I am beginning to realize that my particular mix of gifts is about the least relevant aspect of that call. God led us here first and foremost to learn neighbor-love and to apply it in situations where it is relatively welcome. We've been called to join a weavers' guild, laboring over a masterpiece called the Lowell Neighborhood. We will not settle for cheap solutions that, like my machine-made tapestry that cost neither much sweat nor much money, ultimately will not last or satisfy.

We don't do the weaving especially well. This kind of love is learned, and our apprenticeship has only begun. Many in the church today could easily learn how to do it better. But we now see that the first step is the most important: just getting past all the barriers and taking the plunge, becoming neighbors here. All the rest is added as you go. We are called to follow Jesus' example of incarnational ministry. But living out the Incarnation, as Eugene Peterson has so appropriately captured the essence of it, is as practical and mundane as choosing one's place to live. For "the Word became flesh and moved into the neighborhood" (Jn 1:14 The Message).[14]

Questions for Reflection or Discussion

1. Today's urban problems are complex and interwoven. In what ways might this indicate why purely political solutions or the infusion of funds into today's cities seems not to work?

2. In what way might God be calling you or your group to pick up a strand of yarn and take a place at the loom? What might be a good first step? (See appendix 2.)

7/Songs of the City

◼

The best songs are stories.
—ANONYMOUS
The best stories are songs.
—ANONYMOUS

I HAVE SPENT THE PREVIOUS CHAPTERS INVITING THE READER TO ACcompany my family on our journey to the center of the city, believing that our story demonstrates how God takes very unspectacular people and uses them on an important mission field. The process has been autobiographical, and I've devoted lots of energy to interpreting our experience. But now it is time to let the city define the song, telling what it knows through the power of the experiences it gives to those who minister there.

I have asked several of my friends and colleagues who live and work in Lowell to join me in relaying what we are learning from the city. Some of the stories and poems that follow represent my own untrained "baritone." A few soprano and alto parts were submitted by my friends over the phone or in writing, and I've done some arranging to fit them into the score. What we have all experienced, and what I now retell, have become ballads in the best sense of the word: simple songs or poems telling a story. Their lyrics and melodies have a message for each of us. What follows is an urban musical collection: songs of the city that reveal beauty and truth.

Lullaby: Jesus with Skin

Jodie, a college student at Fresno State, shared this story with me, and I narrate it here using mostly her words.

Late in the day, Jodie knocked on the rotted wooden door, anxiously waiting to see Brenda and the vibrant smiles of her five children. After having met them through an urban project, Jodie had spent many days visiting this family on the west side of town where poverty and violence are the norm. She had earned the love and respect of Brenda and her children so much that they regarded her as a family member. But on this day, she opened the door to a world she had never seen before.

Brenda stared out through the screen with swollen and bloodshot eyes. The only word that came out was "Jodie . . ." as she broke down and sobbed. Jodie came in and hugged her tightly, glancing over her shoulder to survey the room. The house was a mess! Broken beer bottles were strewn on the floor. A large knife lay menacingly on the kitchen counter. Clothes were scattered about.

Brenda's children, screaming in pain, crawled out to see Jodie. They held up their bare feet to her, bloody from the broken glass. Jodie pulled out shard after shard, speaking soothingly to them as she cleaned them up.

When Brenda gained composure, she sat down on her ripped couch and explained what had happened. It was a repeat of an experience that had happened many times before. Brenda's live-in boyfriend had become enraged, thrown things around, beaten Brenda and threatened to kill her, and stormed out—just minutes before Jodie's arrival. The five children, who were all from different fathers, had experienced this all too often from different men.

The paralyzing fear and confusion were overwhelming. Brenda had no resources to prop her up: no job, no stable friends, not many possessions. That night, seeing that God was her only hope, she knelt and wept before him. Jodie sat beside her in humility and awe as this trembling, needy, broken person looked in dependent hope to her Creator.

The children came out into the living room and asked if Jodie could tuck them in. She followed them back to their bedroom. Mindful that the enraged boyfriend might return at any minute, she nevertheless determined to stay and help the children pour out their hearts to God. They formed a circle and held hands as Jodie led them in prayer. They thanked God for being alive, for dying for them, for loving them. After the amen they sang "Jesus Loves Me." Then Jodie helped them crawl into their beds—five mattresses laid out on the dirty floor.

The contrasts were almost too great. These children had witnessed a terrifying fight and had seen their mother threatened and immobilized by fear. Yet an amazing calm had fallen on that little circle, and the peace of Jesus was being pressed into their hearts and minds as Jodie tenderly connected them with each other and their God.

The house was quiet and at peace when Jodie left that night, vastly different from the way she had found it. She understood that God had led her to be there just an instant after the violent boyfriend left, to be "Jesus with skin," as she likes to say, so they weren't alone in the aftermath of something so traumatic. She continues to be there for them. This was (and is) the city's lullaby: Jesus comes alongside.

Trumpet Call: Conveniently Deaf

The gun battle in our neighborhood, a short time after we moved in, vividly brought to mind my previous attitude toward the problems of the city. And I realized that, within a week of moving in, our attitudes and lives had been changed forever. I found myself processing the event in the language of the heart.

Sleeping with the Fan on High

There was a shootout around the corner from my house last night.
Guns popped with the most unlethal sound.

Young men with baggy pants down to their knees
Yelled "Did ya get 'im? Did ya get 'im?"
Bullets ripped past my friend's house and died in a field.
Was there human death too?
Police floodlights and loudspeakers bludgeoned the night
With a brutality not that different from the shooting and shouting.
Rival gangs, they say.
But because we had the fan on a noisy "high" in our room
We missed the whole thing.
Slept through it.
My friend told me.

Instead, we rose to a stunningly clear and cool morning.
We sat on our wide porch and let the faint chill of a
Gentle Sunday breeze nudge us peacefully awake.
We breakfasted on coffee and croissants;
Watched the steam from them rise in a
Brilliant morning light which filled the kitchen.
And while the mothers of slain or imprisoned youths
Wrung their hands in the gnawing grayness of dawn
Ours were folded in the thankful bliss of unknowing.
It's only our first week here in the inner city.
We moved here to "make a difference."
But we haven't decided yet for the future
Whether we'll sleep with a fan or not.
Fact is, I've had the "fan on high"
Most of my life,
Conveniently deaf to the cries of pain around me.
It's easier not knowing;
Not knowing is a hard habit to break.

Dirge: Aurelio's Last Walk Home

Aurelio was a nice boy. Growing up in the poorest neighborhood of
Fresno had certainly shaped him, but it had not misshaped him as of
yet. Some of his friends were joining gangs, but not Aurelio. Kim

Taylor, an inner-city missionary, had invested in him through Bible clubs when Aurelio was younger. But now that he was in junior high he came to them less frequently. Two things distinguished Aurelio among those who knew him. One was his bright smile and playful spirit, both of which he would flash at the least provocation. The other was his pet opossum who went with him everywhere. We all got such a kick out of this unlikely pet—such a country animal in the heart of the city—that whenever we said Aurelio's name the opossum got a mention too.

One afternoon, as Kim drove through the streets of Lowell picking up kids for a special event, she came upon Aurelio playing with some friends. It had been a while since she had seen him, so she stopped to talk. He was busy with his friends, so Kim hesitated to ask him to come to the event that night. But at the last minute she asked them all. The others weren't interested, but Aurelio paused and then said, "Okay, I'd like to come." His friends thought it was uncool, but Aurelio's decision was made. That evening, he clearly heard the gospel presented in a way that boys his age could understand. Kim wasn't sure how he was responding to the message, but he had fun that evening.

Less than a week later Kim got a call from one of the girls in the neighborhood saying that Aurelio had been shot, apparently as he engaged in the dangerous and high-risk activity of . . . walking home from school. As he turned a corner he came upon two gangs who were firing on each other with handguns. He ran, but one of the bullets found him anyway. He died the next day.

Many of the Christian families who had moved into the neighborhood to do ministry surrounded Aurelio's family with love and support. Kim and her colleagues at World Impact helped Aurelio's friends process the experience and supported them with love. As a result of the shooting, the junior high school he attended finally instituted a program of adult crossing guards and supervisors to monitor the key streets for a mile around the campus. And kids, many of them from the gangs, attended the funeral and heard about this innocent boy with the pet opossum who was cut down at the age of twelve. Aurelio's death has become a symbol of the brokenness of this city.

For Kim, this city-song was difficult and powerful. This was the city's funeral dirge reminding us that relationships are precious. We cannot take them for granted. We do not know what tomorrow holds. Every moment shared intentionally with a child in need is an investment which may have eternal consequences. And God is very much a part of that process. After all, this awesome God whom Kim serves had orchestrated a way for Aurelio to hear the gospel a few days before his death. She's hoping to see that bright smile again.

Our family met Aurelio only once. He was playing with his next-door neighbor's computer. The neighbors are Christians; in fact, they're one of the families in the network—they moved here to make a difference. We were at their home for a potluck, and there was Aurelio with his pet opossum crawling up and down his shoulder. What a funny sight! When we learned of his death we realized that if we hadn't met him, he would have merely been another statistic in the city's growing murder list. In that brief conversation he became human, real enough to make him more than just a statistic.

It was his opossum that endeared him to us, and it was his opossum that got me meditating on how crazy-upside-down our world is, where children are terrorizing each other and holding whole cities hostage to fear. What follows came out of that meditation.

Opossum Mourns Aurelio

From upside down I saw him live
Aurelio my friend.
A city kid, just twelve years old,
No one could guess his end.

On mornings bright I'd hear him come
To pet my ropey tail.
Upon his neck he'd carry me
And chart a wand'ring trail.

Opossums are but country things
The city is like fire.
And my boys' street a tangle of
Protected turf and ire.

An unsafe place of things more cruel
Than darkest jungles wild:
Of human young with ashen hearts
Whose days and nights are guile.

He'd carry me to neighbors next
Who spoke of love and hope,
Whose kindnesses embraced us both
And warmed Aurelio.

So upside down I traveled on
This road from fear to love.
From love to fear and back again
He'd hoist me up above.

Until the day this path left him
Fallen on the ground.
Wrong place, wrong time, a brutal deed
And horror all around.

I see the world a certain way,
My vantage wrong way round.
But when boys kill boys
Opossum asks:
Whose world is upside down?

March: Why Would Someone Oppose a Good Thing?

Just as I was climbing into bed late one night the phone rang, and I
rose with a sense of foreboding to answer it. The last two days had
been a struggle, and I was tired. It had been a wrestling match with

discouragement and intimidation over the process of trying to assist transformation in Lowell. Somehow I knew this call would be related.

The person on the phone wanted to let me know that there was a determined effort on the part of "certain people" who were active in neighborhood and city politics to stifle and undermine any effort sponsored by Christians in the neighborhood, in some cases without even cursory consideration. Apparently they were feeling threatened and "weren't going to let Christians take over." Since the group of Christian agencies we were working with had no intention of "taking over," but only of joining the process and of training college students in loving and serving this neighborhood of pain, the accusation was absurd. But then, so were many aspects of the process of local government into which I have been baptized as we have tried to bring health and hope to this part of the city. Naively, we never expected that picking up trash, painting houses, tutoring at-risk schoolchildren, providing streetlights and making sure that city dollars earmarked for this area really go to this area would be met with any opposition. And because it makes no sense, it was a reminder that *other* powers are at work here too.

Hearing the military-march cadences and battle lyrics of this city-song has humbled us. We see how far the systems of the city have been influenced by the evil and deceitfulness of the human heart, and it has led us to tears. This is what Nehemiah must have felt as Governor Sanballat sought to thwart his efforts to rebuild the city of Jerusalem and restore the people there. And that is what Jesus felt. After all, he wept over what he saw in the city. Maybe tears are what we need. The battle songs of the city are often sad. The city is worth crying over.

Fiddle Tune: The Snickerdoodle Strategy

The street was especially dark as we stood there in the night chill. The knowledge that this was the home turf of the "College Street Locals," an inner-city Fresno gang, made me rethink the wisdom of what we were doing. What were fifteen very middle-class, wide-eyed college seniors doing standing at the door of an inner-city home in a violent neighborhood at night, holding a plate of snickerdoodles and singing

"Jesus loves us, this we know"? We looked incredibly vulnerable. But before I had the time to question the wisdom of it all, Mable, the elderly woman who lived there, finally answered the door with surprise and delight on her face.

Why were we there? I had told my students that we were baking snickerdoodles and delivering them to encourage people in the neighborhood. "Snickerdoodles can open doors," I said. But deep down I knew that the ones delivering the treats would themselves be treated to a new vision of life by getting out into this neighborhood. It's the Snickerdoodle Strategy. The first task in giving Christians a vision for meeting this world with the gospel is the task of helping them *see* the needs that exist. Once we truly see, then we can fashion appropriate forms of response.

Our group had been studying how bringing good news to the poor and binding up the brokenhearted are at the very heart of the gospel. That night we had just finished looking at Isaiah 61, the passage Jesus quotes in Luke 4 when introducing his ministry. It defines ministry to the poor as being central to his identity and mission. We were doing more than delivering cookies. We were continuing the ministry of Jesus on earth as he defined his call. If anybody was poor, brokenhearted and a captive, certainly Mable was.

Mable's story is typical. She had been trapped. Unable to sell and get out of a changing neighborhood when all of her friends did, she watched as it became a center for drugs, chaotic youth and violence. Because there was no one to stand with her, together providing a model for stable life in the neighborhood, she stood alone. Christians had fled as well, removing the role models and restraints with which praying believers infuse their surroundings by their very presence. Eventually she responded by becoming embittered and alienating herself from her new neighbors, and that only made the problem worse.

What she needed on this dark night was Christians to stand at her side—and even some to "reneighbor" her part of the city by relocating to it. She needed the image of a gang of students armed with snickerdoodles and singing "Jesus Loves Me" to replace the visions of gangs with AK-47s that haunt her nights. We hold our study at my house, just around the corner from Mable's. Since it is my neighborhood too, I understand her fear. But unlike Mable, my family and I are here with lots of support and a vision for partnering with others to spark change there.

As my students and alumni stood there, I knew that real education was happening. One of the people in my group is a new teacher at an inner-city Fresno junior high school, the school to which many gang kids from that neighborhood go. That night, as Mable stood beaming over the plate of snickerdoodles before her, Stacey the teacher saw a tangible example of the sociology of fear. Here was a glimpse of the environment that her students come from, and it was an open door to comprehending the root needs in their lives. She returned to her school the following week with a more complete picture of her task as a Christian teacher in a public school.

That night the city was singing an upbeat, stomp-your-feet, square-dance tune about the power of encouragement as an antidote to fear. Snickerdoodles and sidewalk serenades produced encouragement and perspective that night. Powerful little cookie.

Country-Western: The Power of an Average Love

Jodie shared another story, and again I retell it using mostly her words:

Jodie got some practice at being a sister while she was growing up—but not like she's getting these days. As a college student, she is involved in the InterVarsity Christian Fellowship chapter at her university, holds down a part-time job, keeps her academic commitments and still carves out precious time to be an older sister to the children of two inner-city families whom she met on an urban project. It's an avocation that consumes a lot of emotional energy. It has saved at least one life, redeemed another and provided hope in hopeless situations. But Jodie would be the first to tell you that what she does is not spectacular. Its power comes from the fact that she employs a level of love common to all Christians. The circumstances themselves are not average. But it is an ordinary love that she so powerfully applies there.

One family in particular has been changed forever because of Jodie's focused servanthood and love. In a tutoring program Jodie met Corina, eleven years old and living in Lowell. Soon after, Jodie visited her at home at Christmas time, only to be met by the grandmother standing in the doorway weeping. Corina's father had just been murdered in a drug deal gone bad. That initial contact symbolized the kind of encounters Jodie would have in the next two years as she invested in that family.

When Corina's older sister got pregnant and was thinking about an abortion, Jodie's love and companionship convinced her to have the baby and offer it for adoption. Jodie even coached the delivery. A life was saved.

She spent nights at Corina's house, building friendship and trust. Soon Corina began to share the real story of what happens on the streets. She confided in Jodie about the pressure to "make the run" or "jump in" to a gang. Jodie began to understand the need for Corina to have some semblance of family, even if the sense of "family" which the gang offered was even more dysfunctional than her own. Hers had been torn apart by poverty, poor education, the drug addiction of the mother and now the murder of the father. The gang was another version of this upheaval, but at least membership included a sense of belonging with other kids in her circumstances.

Jodie tells the story of one night when she took Corina to the movies, two years into their relationship. When it was time to go home, she hopped into her car, strapped on her seat belt and waited for Corina to get in. Instead, Corina disappeared into a gang- and drug-infested apartment complex where all the lighting had been shot out. Jodie called for her and contemplated going in to look for her. But an approaching policeman warned her not to. "Do you like living?" he asked. "Then don't go in there."

Nervous and afraid, Jodie asked him to be on the lookout for Corina, then began to drive all the streets in that neighborhood. Anger, fear and betrayal rose up in her as she searched. What had happened to all the trust she had earned over the last two years? Hadn't she prayed, spent nights there, given of herself, given her very heart? Yet Corina still ran.

Slowly it came to Jodie what had happened. It had been time to go home, and Corina had not wanted to return to the harsh home environment that she hated, that she couldn't handle, that she shouldn't have to handle. As Jodie drove fearfully past the drug deals, the prostitutes and the gangs at two a.m., her resentment turned to understanding. Not finding Corina anywhere, she released her to God and slowly drove home.

She attempted further contact, but Corina was on the streets for over a month. Her grandmother had no word. Jodie went home for the summer, wrote letters, never received an answer.

Upon her return to school, she dropped by to see if Corina had returned. She had—and she ran to Jodie excitedly as she came through the door. She asked if they could go on a long drive to talk, which they did.

"Jodie, I'm home again," Corina shared. "I've been on those streets for a long time, but not no more. I'm back." She went on to describe life on the streets, the shelters and gang houses where she slept, what she ate, etc. "Jodie, you know what? I was gonna join that gang, but I didn't. I told them about you and they got all mad. I said you're like a sister to me and to join them would be turning my back on you. I couldn't do that. I was about to do the run [where the person who is being initiated in a gang has to run through a line of gang members while they beat him or her], but then I said, 'Why should I fight for their acceptance when I know that God and Jodie love me, and I don't have to prove nothin'?' So I walked away. And you know what else? I know you don't do no drugs, so I didn't do none either on the streets. And, will you help me get back in school again?"

Jodie wept with joy and thankfulness. Her persistence had paid off. All those talks had registered with Corina. Loving Corina with her average, nonglitzy, persistent love had produced amazing results. Corina had come back to her family and to Jesus.

This was the city's "country music"—a saga of sin, love, betrayal and return. But more than that, this ballad is about a young woman who, in her spare time and with a very basic and average understanding of love, rubbed off on a very broken urban family. The city sings a song that says, "Average love wields an incredible power here. Anyone can do it."

Blues: A Plausible Panic

One night, a woman from our neighborhood appeared with her two small children on our doorstep in tears. Pam told us that they had been thrown violently out of her apartment by her drunken roommate, a woman she had trusted. Her two babies hadn't been fed and they needed diapers. We brought her into our home, went to a friend's house to get some diapers, cradled her baby and comforted her. My boys played with her toddler. We gave her the numbers to places that could help with both short-term and longer-term housing. She was able to stay with her grandmother overnight. Finally, we prayed for her. All the while, one of the students who lives with us was watching this—and learning. It occurred to me that we were living out our vision for being here: both direct ministry to the poor and training in compassion for college students.

A week later, as one of my students and I walked in Lowell at dusk, I was surprised to see Pam on the corner. She approached me but obviously didn't recognize me. She began a story very similar to the one she had tearfully related just the week before at my house. I stopped her short, saying, "Pam, it's me, Randy. Remember?" We talked for a moment more, and it became clear to me that we had been used by someone who had lots of practice looking plausible in her "panic."

Yet even this became part of the tapestry God is weaving. It gave us the chance to understand the cycles so many poor people are locked into. It gave us the chance to reevaluate the motivations behind our noble service to the needy in this neighborhood. And it gave us the chance to ask ourselves whether we were going to live closed, suspicious lives or whether we would be willing to be taken, conned and lied to for Jesus' sake.

This city-song had the low and rhythmic twang of the blues, a form of music loved for its simplicity and pathos but even more for its ability to describe reality.

Sing-along Round: The Patience of the Poor
For months an inner-city ministry in Fresno had been planning and recruiting for a retreat with families. Brenda, a staffworker, was really excited about building relationships with them and knitting them together with one another, creating a community which would provide the foundation for renewal in the Lowell Neighborhood. But an hour into the trip the bus carrying most of the families broke down on I-5, a hot and dusty thoroughfare. They clearly wouldn't make it to their destination; in fact, they were going to miss the first day entirely. Then, as one of the vans carrying other families circled back to the bus, it was sideswiped. The sense of worry was compounding in the staff team, and Brenda wondered if they should abort the whole thing. Maybe it wasn't meant to be.

She and the rest of the staff team looked at the families on the bus and said, "What should we do? Maybe, in light of all that has happened, we should turn around and go home."

But the men on the bus said, "No! No one is hurt. Let's fix the bus!" Before long, auto parts were strewn beside the bus and men had grease up to their elbows. The atmosphere was like a party as men worked from above and below the engine, some grunting to loosen a bolt, some handing tools, some joking. After a while, it became clear that the problem was too great to repair on the roadside, and the staff began shuttling vanloads to the retreat center. There were no complaints. Even as the men worked on the bus, the moms and kids went to a nearby 7-11 store and got Big Gulps. It was still a vacation. Eventually everyone made it to the retreat, and the goal of the weekend was wonderfully realized.

As the staff reflected on the incident later, some interesting insights emerged. A more middle-class busload might have reacted differently, seeing the breakdown as an unwelcome intrusion on the weekend, an inconvenience that "ruined everything." But those who are poor often find their older cars breaking down on the road. It is all part of the adventure. It is to be accepted. Any break from their routine, especially when it involves other people, is seen as a chance to celebrate. Inconveniences are all part of the territory.

   This city-song was like the rounds families sing to pass the time on a long trip in the car. It was an urban "Row, Row, Row Your Boat," celebrating the patience of the poor, their ability to take life as it comes and to center their happiness in relationships—being together—rather than in a well-ordered existence.

Anthem: Growing Larger

I include this last poem because it reflects a little of the motivation which drew us to the city. It was written as we moved. It is a song about hope and about being called to something larger than ourselves. It is about becoming larger. It is about the city helping us become more human, more full of the life God intended.

   Moving Down to Move Up

   Packing all but the now broken habit of mediocre dreams
   I load the car with hope as well as boxes.
   With shy smiles we brush off the astonishment of gaping neighbors
   And those who shake their heads in a comfortable
   Concern for our welfare, or disdain for our naiveté.
   One last look at what has been our home
   And we embark with a prayer for our new address in the
      "evil inner city."
   No, we are happily not in our right minds.
   We look full in the face of something so un-American,
   A chosen downward mobility,
   An intentional dwelling with "the poor," and
   We see only blessing.

   It's a big house, the house we move to,
   with room enough for joy and suffering,
   Housemates and laughter, anguish and empty spaces;
   An unpoor place in a neighborhood of pain;
   A home and a street with dimension,
   With human needs close and large enough to help us

Feel both our smallness and our significance;
A life where love is both
Mission and survival.
Some cultures shrink heads
As trophy of the conqueror.
Ours shrinks the heart—
Its place reduced to mere function,
Its pulse weak with puny aspirations.
We are hollow, anemic,
Drowning in dullness,
Oblivious to the undermining of the soul.
Perhaps what beats in me, distracted and shallow,
Can regrow downtown, in that fertile desert of a place
Where wildflowers split concrete—
Can regrow to pound in my chest the full
Rhythms of love and of life
Loud enough to hear,
Beckoning all to the One who left His home
For us.

Music Appreciation

Most of us stick with the kind of music that we grew up with. We tend not to venture out much beyond the styles we began to develop a taste for early in our youth. That, of course, is where the generation gap between parents and children becomes most visible. But the songs of the city are timeless, and they are sung through people who are as different from each other as Nat King Cole and Kurt Cobain were. The diverse rhythms, unfamiliar harmonies, dark interludes and joyous crescendos set us "humming" new thoughts and intoning new strategies which, when mixed with faith, could change the urban world. This has become true for us, and we can't stop singing.

Questions for Reflection or Discussion
1. What kinds of songs are prevalent in your life these days?

2. What feelings are present in you as you read the "songs of the city" in this chapter?

3. Some of the best literary creations in history are beautiful precisely for their sadness. Consider the book of Lamentations in the Old Testament. What kind of song might God himself be singing when he looks at the state of the inner city today?

4. What part might you sing if you were to join the chorus of people across the country who are singing a new song for the city?

Epilogue: Journey of a Thousand Miles

Our journey from the suburbs to the Lowell Neighborhood was only about six miles. Though it took three days for Jonah to walk across Nineveh, an overweight, chain-smoking jogger could weave his way from one end of Fresno to the other in the space of a morning. But to many of our friends it might as well have been a journey of a thousand miles from our cozy three-bedroom, two-bath suburban house to the crazy old boarding house we now call home. No matter that it is filled tonight with howls of laughter from neighborhood women who have gathered to support each other and hear from the Lord. For most, it seems like a *very* risky trip.

But for others it's no big deal. We have neighbors who lived here long before we moved. Right next door to us are Bill and Becky, who were making a difference by being good neighbors long before it became theologically trendy to speak of "neighbor-love in the inner city." They chose to live here because they love the old part of town with its architectural beauty and uniqueness. They befriend neighbors, love the children, lend tools, come to the aid of those in need—and do it all instinctively, with no special training required. And while we came with a defined vision for community development and urban ministry training, we joined them and others who simply want what is good for our part of this city.

I invited you on this journey for three reasons. First, I wanted you to see the process by which an average middle-class family received a call to give our lives for the welfare of the city. The life we have found here is more accessible, enjoyable and satisfying than anyone (ourselves included) might have thought. Second, I wanted to pass along a vision for the rebuilding of the city (Is 62) and to demonstrate the very average ways transformation happens in and through the fabric of our life here. And third, I wanted to testify that God has provided all that we have needed as we ventured out in faith on this journey. He is faithful!

Flying On
On this journey we've learned some things. As we said in chapter one, "flying upside down" makes you look at life differently. Amazingly, this inverted worldview has helped to clarify the things we truly value. And while the things we want in life have changed, we are getting the things we now want!

And we're not alone. Our little aircraft has taken on passengers, and other planes have fallen into formation in a wonderful "return flight." Just this month another group of students has inhabited a large pink house in the heart of downtown and is pledged to grow as leaders there, learn biblical community and engage in urban ministry. These are college students, with academic loads, jobs, friendships and ministry responsibilities, who have gained a heart for the city and have taken the first step on an amazing journey.

The Rooms of My House
Those who embark on this journey will certainly find that God is involved every step of the way. As we described in chapter two, he will not only find you the right address; he will also be in charge of the renovation process—both the renovation that happens in the house

and the one that happens in your heart.

Did you ever read that little booklet *My Heart—Christ's Home?*[1] In it, Bob Munger pictures Jesus walking through and transforming various rooms of a person's life. First he goes through "the library," representing the mind, the control room of each individual. He enters the "drawing room"—we might call it the family room. This is the place of fellowship with Christ, representing our spiritual life. Then it's on to "the workshop," the places in our life where we should be bearing fruit for the kingdom. After that it's "the play room," which is where we spend our leisure time. Finally he demands to see the "hall closet," representing the secret places of our lives. Jesus goes through all of these rooms and transforms them into what he originally intended them to be.

This is the very thing we have found happening, almost by default, as we have accepted the call to the city. Our lives as well as our new home are looking better all the time.

An Involved Point of View

Once we were in the city, it was hard *not* to behold it with new eyes, to see it with clarity and appreciation. But in our preparation for the move, we discovered that there are ways to behold the city realistically even before making such a move. (Appendix 2 gives a list of twenty-one things a group or individual can do to increase involvement in the city before attempting relocation.)

And realism is important. We must somehow avoid the sin of Jonah. When God called him to go to a people whom he feared and despised, he took his culture's equivalent of the Concorde jet in the opposite direction. He saw only a people and a nation worth condemning. He did not see the humanness and dignity that certainly existed as they do in all cultures; he did not see even the children (those who do not know their right hand from their left) of that great city crying out for their God.

Exposure and involvement have taught us that there is much to love even in the most difficult neighborhoods. Part of our ability to come to that realization is a result of the face-to-face dismantling of our erroneous and negative stereotypes about the city.

Neighbor-Love

Getting there is one thing. Learning to live there as neighbors intent on building the kingdom is another. Neighbor-love is a learned activity. At one point in our nation's history it came more naturally. Communities were closer-knit: neighbors knew each other's names; life situations didn't change much over whole lifetimes. Of course, that could be bad or good, often depending on things like social class, ethnicity and job skills. And the context of stability that created the kind of environment where neighbor-love *could* flourish was no guarantee that it *would*.

But love of neighbor these days has to operate in the context of a highly mobile culture of self-focused, individualized people who regard personal security and pleasure as their highest birthright. It's not the best training ground. I am suggesting that the city (especially in its neediest neighborhoods, where crime, poverty, dysfunctionality and brokenness go unchecked) is simultaneously the best training ground for Christians to learn love of neighbor and the place where love of neighbor makes the most profound and immediate impact.

Family Affair

As we have lived our lives now for several years in just such an environment, we have found a clear sense of mission as a family. Our life is organized around it. It filters into our children's prayers over meals and before bedtime. It floats into our students' conversations. It frames our schedules, and it defines our options for us. It is not an addition to our family life. It is part and parcel of it. We are learning a kingdom ethic that says we are not our own but belong body and soul to our Savior. Here is where life is to be found (Mk 8:35).

Making Music

As we clarified our family's purpose, the thought arose that our lives were, in fact, "songs" in the making. This is so true. The years are like musical scores. Every day notes are added, sometimes in upbeat major keys, sometimes in brooding minor chords. And when we come to the end of life, the eulogies said at our funerals summarize our lives and become the lyrics of the song. The epitaphs on our gravestones are the song titles.

With this in mind we began to desire the song titles of our lives to be more than these: "He got his college degree," "She was fully employed," "They had a family," "Their children got degrees and found jobs." We wanted the songs of our lives to be about something more lasting—something eternal. Our move to Lowell expanded these songs as we let the city sing to us through our new life rhythms and experiences. It is a constant music, a symphony backdrop to our lives.

Key to the Journey: Crossing Paths

Remember the Duncans, our friends we met in Oxford who were on sabbatical from their mission in urban Manila, the ones who taught us to fly upside down? When we met them, the Duncans were on a journey of their own. It was the journey of their evolving call—from doing community development and church planting in some of the poorest neighborhoods in the world to teaching and training others to do it as well. And herein lies the key to understanding our story. *Their* journey intersected with *our* journey and changed it forever. This, in the simplest and purest terms, is all we are doing now. Our journey to the center of our city is, in the final analysis, merely an attempt to cross paths with those who are poor and those who care about the poor, allowing our lives to influence one another, providing new contexts where Jesus Christ can make something happen—something new and redemptive—both in their lives and in ours.

A New Raphael

When this path-crossing happens, it's amazing how normal it feels. For example, one afternoon little eight-year-old Raphael, a child from our neighborhood, wandered into my office from the living room where he had been playing with my sons. I always smile when I see him. Since I was raised around the world of art, I love his name. The classic paintings by his namesake often focus on biblical scenes. This little Raphael always looks at me with a twinkle in his eye. Maybe it's a response to my smile. Maybe it's just a response to the candy I often have. I suspect, though, it's the attention I pay to him.

Today he asks me what I'm doing. I show him the computer screen. I spell C-A-T and D-O-G for him. Though he is in the second grade, he cannot read these words. It is so typical of this neighborhood. What crushes me today, though, is his attitude of defeat and resignation about his inability to read. He has nearly given up. I call his teacher to get a feel for how we can help him. She says just read to him. So that's what we are doing: reading, including, loving.

Cindy, one of the students living and partnering with us, reaches out to him through our Wise Old Owl Reading Club for children in the neighborhood. It is where we link college students with Lowell schoolchildren. Recently Raphael helped her make cookies for the club. The look of pride in his eyes as he held the mixer was worth a million bucks!

The first time we met, nine months earlier, he was galloping on my porch, jumping off and leading a pack of roving seven-year-olds in the same. They were out of control, little wolves, sweating in their wildness and careless in their seven-year-old arrogance. But now, when I come to the door, he hugs me. This eight-year-old boy hugs me as a toddler would. And he sits quietly beside me while I show him what a computer does.

The other day as Raphael sat next to me in his normal position, out of the blue he said to me, "Randy, what are you?"

I said, "Well, I'm like a pastor."

He said, "What's a pastor?"

"Well," I said, "I help people learn about Jesus and how much he loves us."

"Is that like God?" Raphael responded.

"Yes, Raphael, I show people how to love God and how to go to heaven."

He thought about that for a moment. Then, with his famous smile growing from the left corner of his mouth and his eyes sparkling, the color of liquid chocolate, he looked up at me and asked, "Can I go there?"

"Would you like to?" I asked.

He said, "Yes!" and with that we prayed, right there in the glow of the computer screen. As Raphael repeated "Amen" after me he smiled and said, "Can we play a computer game now?"

Nothing of this conversation or of our growing relationship is spectacular. Raphael is very poor. His home situation as I have come to know it is incredibly unstable. But this little boy's life is being slowly, steadily changed by the normal interactions brought on by our being his neighbor. The students living with us have noticed the change. They are being mentored in the ways of transformation. It's hard to miss. From a sweaty "I don't care" to interested dialogue. From out-of-control wildness to heartfelt hugs. All in nine months. Interesting, isn't it? Gestation. From a fertilized egg to a gasping baby. From an angel's announcement to a straw-filled manger. All in nine months.

If you have made it to the final page of this literary journey, I wonder what God is doing in your heart. Perhaps it is time for you to prayerfully ask yourself, *Is there something stirring in me, making me want to deal seriously with the plight of the city and to embody God's love for the people there?*

It is said that the longest journey of all is the one that stretches from the *head* to the *heart*. And as in all journeys, even the famous "journey of a thousand miles," the trip begins with a first step. Whether God leads you to "fly upside down" by joining the relocation movement or not is up to him. Certainly we are all called to follow him where he is going. We are called to be his children, living out the will and the values of our Father (Jn 14:21). In light of this, I wonder if it might help you to ask this final question. *Could it be that I cannot know what my role is in God's agenda for the healing of the city, for the building of his kingdom and for the transforming of my life, until I take that first responsive step? What might that step be for me?*

Questions for Reflection or Discussion

1. Which "room" of your life might God be wanting to renovate? Is there a neighborhood of your city where the needs are great and where God might want to plant a team of Christians?

2. Which of the stereotypes of the city discussed in this book might God be calling you to reexamine in your life?

3. Where are you practicing neighbor-love in your life? What does it look like?

4. If you could draw something to symbolize what you want your life or your family's life to stand for, what would you draw?

5. What song is your life writing right now? How might the city influence the notes or the lyrics you are now forming?

Appendix 1

Bible Studies on God and the City for Individuals or Groups
The following eleven Bible studies (some very brief, some longer) focus on various issues surrounding God's redemptive action toward the city. Some deal with the issue of rebuilding the city itself. Others deal with issues of righteousness; justice for the poor; the emotional considerations of looking honestly at the challenge of the city. They are designed to help you go deeper in applying Scripture to today's world and its needs.

Study 1: The Heart of Jesus and the Potential of the Poor
Isaiah 61:1-4; 62:1-12

Before you study: Spend a few minutes writing out your answer to this question, and then read it to someone and ask whether is is clear and complete: Why did Jesus come?

1. Read Isaiah 61:1-2. Sound familiar? Where else in the Bible have you encountered these words?

2. Read Luke 4:18-19. Why would Jesus choose this text to define his mission and purpose?

3. What are the key words in Jesus' purpose statement in Luke, and what clues do they give us about the nature of his mission? Back in the Isaiah passage, what people are the primary benefici-

aries of the Messiah's mission?

4. Read Isaiah 61:3-4. What vision does the Messiah have for who these people will become? What name does God give them?

5. How is that vision different from how most of our city regards the potential of "the poor"?

6. Read Isaiah 62:1-7. What is God's attitude toward Jerusalem in verses 1-3?

7. What names describe Jerusalem?

8. What names are used to describe your city?

9. What vision does God have for what Jerusalem will become? What names will he give it?

10. What part does he want the faithful in Jerusalem to play in bringing all this to pass (vv. 6-7)? What does it mean to take no rest and give the Lord no rest?

11. Read verses 8-12. What is the source of hope for the city of Jerusalem? (Notice that when the Savior comes to the city it gets a new name.)

12. As New Testament believers, we have Jesus in us. What method does God use to allow the hope of the Messiah to penetrate our city? List some ways in which Jesus' description of his mission can be a guide for us as we seek to live out his agenda in this world.

Study 2: What Does It Mean to Know God (as He Has Defined Knowing)?
Jeremiah 22

Background: On the surface, this chapter appears to be a series of judgments against evil kings of Judah. But it really is about God's heart for the city and for the poor. The reforms the good King Josiah had enacted in the nation had "officially" returned Judah to the worship of Yahweh. But the hearts of the people had, to a large degree, remained unchanged. Upon Josiah's death, his son, King Jehoiakim, abandoned the righteous ways of his father that had benefited the people, and the nation had official sanction again to abandon God. Jehoiakim would simply pursue luxury and the benefits of power. But he received this profound rebuke and ominous prophecy from the Lord he had abandoned, and in the midst of it we catch a glimpse of what is on the heart of God.

1. Read Jeremiah 22. How would you characterize the tone of this passage? What might this tone tell us about how God feels about what he is saying?

2. Look specifically at verses 1-12. King Shallum succeeded his father Josiah but did not continue his father's just reign. What does God want from the king? Make a list.

3. What are the consequences of the king's not mirroring what is on the heart of God?

4. Look specifically at verses 13-19. King Jehoiakim, Shallum's older brother, became king and took the nation and the throne to a new low. What was important to Jehoiakim (vv. 13-14, 17), and how far was he willing to go to get it?

5. Look at the first question asked in verse 15.

☐ What is the Lord saying to Jehoiakim by his sarcastic tone?

☐ In contrast to what Jehoiakim obviously believed, where are the security and comfort of a king supposed to come from?

☐ What similar mistake do we as a culture make as we live our lives in the secular work force?

6. Look at the second question asked in verse 15. The Lord contrasts Jehoiakim with his father Josiah.

☐ What point is God making?

☐ In what ways do *we* need to consider this point?

7. Josiah is described in verses 15-16. What was he like?

8. God asks, regarding the righteous actions of Josiah on behalf of the poor and oppressed, "Isn't *that* what it means to *know me?*"

☐ How does this statement compare with our often highly spiritualized definitions of knowing God?

☐ What might be some ways that we could "know God" better on *his* terms, that is, as he has defined it here?

9. In our highly pluralistic world, where truth is seen as relative, how might a church group or fellowship of Christian students who defined "knowing God" in Jeremiah's terms and were involved in hands-on ministries of compassion and advocacy for the poor be

regarded? In other words, how might *doing* the gospel help people see the truth of the gospel?

10. Look at verses 18-30.

□ What was Jehoiakim's fate?

□ What legacy did he leave behind?

11. With all the good *things* available in our culture, Americans can be among the most wasteful and materialistic of all peoples. Our lives so often consist of spending and acquiring. We even call ourselves "consumers." Our very identity, the way we see ourselves, is tied up in the consumption of things!

□ How may we resemble Jehoiakim?

□ What kind of legacy will you leave behind—one that resembles the self-centeredness of Jehoiakim or one that resembles the God-centered heart and actions of Josiah? How can you tell which you resemble more?

Study 3: Seeking the Welfare of Babylon
Jeremiah 29:4-7

Background: The nation of Israel has been carried off into captivity. They did not listen to Jeremiah's prophecy, preferring to follow the false prophets who told them everything was okay. Jeremiah now writes a letter to the captive nation in Babylon, revealing God's will for the people. We are in a similar situation. We live in enemy territory, but we are citizens of heaven. Will we obey God's will for us while we are here?

1. Read Jeremiah 29:4-7. What did God command the captives to do? Make a list.

2. What was God's reason for having the Judean exiles pray for Babylon (v. 7)? How do you think they felt about praying for the city of their captors?

3. How do you feel about praying for gang members you read about in the papers? for those in prison for murder? Do you pray for them? Why or why not?

4. What does it mean to "seek the welfare of the city"? Brainstorm some specific examples.

5. Some people today say, "The city is the cesspool of human sin, so we should just abandon it to its own ways and keep our children as far from it as possible." Others say, "Things are predicted to get worse before the Lord comes back, so why seek the welfare of the city? We're just delaying his Second Coming." How does this logic fit with what you know about God's heart for the city as we see it in Scripture and particularly here in Jeremiah?

6. What aspects of your own Babylon do you feel most compelled to pray for? Make a list.

7. What one thing could you or your fellowship group do this week to seek the welfare of your city?

Study 4: Seeing the City with the Eyes of the Heart
Nehemiah 1

Background: Nehemiah, whose name means "The Lord has comforted," probably grew up in captivity. After Babylon had sacked Jerusalem, Persia conquered Babylon. The people of Israel had lived in foreign cities for a generation, with only a poor remnant allowed to stay in Palestine. Nehemiah was placed strategically by God to be the cupbearer, the official food taster, to the king of Persia. But his sense of identity and his historic tie to Jerusalem were evident, as was his faith in God.

1. Read Nehemiah 1. What news did Nehemiah's brother bring about those who survived the exile and about the state of the city of Jerusalem? What words did he use to paint a picture for Nehemiah?

2. The wall of any major city represented more than mere protection, though it certainly did that. It represented the identity of the city. Likewise, the gates of the city were more than entry points. They were the place where the legal system of the city operated; they represented the social coherence and viability of the people. With these things in mind, what was Hanani trying to say to Nehemiah about the city of Jerusalem?

3. What was Nehemiah's first response to the news? Why was he affected this way?

4. Today's cities present the same kind of news that caused Nehemiah to despair. List the things that most discourage you about the

state of your city. Why is it so hard to face these things—to look at them soberly and honestly—and want to do something?

5. How else did Nehemiah respond? How did the spiritual disciplines help him process the news he had received?

6. Take a good look at Nehemiah's prayer in verses 5-11. Why should Nehemiah include himself in confessing the sins of the nation of Israel (sins that resulted in Israel's overthrow) when Nehemiah had been no more than a baby, if born at all, when it happened?

7. Likewise, are there dark things in your city that need to be confessed but that you have not participated in? How do you feel about that?

8. Nehemiah remembers a promise of God and reminds God of it. It is the vision of a once scattered people returning in repentance to God and being returned to their homeland.

9. What clue is there at the end of Nehemiah's prayer that this vision is becoming a plan?

10. Chapter 2 tells of Nehemiah coming to the king with an elaborate plan to rebuild the city of Jerusalem, asking the king for leave and resources to pull it off. What would make Nehemiah want to leave his cushy position in the king's court for such a dangerous journey? Is there a vision of God in your life so compelling that you would be willing to risk comfort and security to carry it out?

Study 5: Integrity and Partnership with the Poor
Nehemiah 5

Background: After chapter 1, Nehemiah was prepared for the time when God would bring the opportunity to present his vision of a rebuilt Jerusalem to the king of Persia. He left his cushy job and embarked on a perilous journey fraught with danger and opposition. He rallied the people to work, overcame discouragement, marshaled resources and kept the vision. He used cunning and creativity in getting people to work on the wall, rebuilding national pride as well. He demonstrated consistent leadership, a prayerful approach to the problems and challenges, and a keen insight into what it takes to turn a scattered people into a family again. Now the wall was rebuilt, and people were having to relearn what God wanted of them as a city and as a nation. Immediately they were faced with a crisis which could have undone everything Nehemiah had worked for.

1. Read Nehemiah 5. Three groups brought complaints to Nehemiah, this new leader they were growing to trust. These groups (summarized by the words *some, others* and *still others*) all had similar complaints. Make a list.

2. Some are hungry. Others have had to become indebted in order to buy food. Still others are having to become indebted and even sell their children into slavery to pay the taxes being forced upon them. These levels of poverty were common, and the rich were exploiting the powerlessness of the people. How does their complaint affect Nehemiah? What's his initial response?

3. After letting himself experience anger over the injustice, and after pondering over it all, he is ready to act. What does he do?

4. Nehemiah is confronting the religious and political leaders of the city—the established power structure. What risk is he taking? How have the powerful in our day typically responded when reproached by those with a moral argument against their behavior?

5. How do the leaders respond to Nehemiah? Why?

6. In verses 14-19 Nehemiah gives a clue to the key to his success with both the leaders and the general populace in the city. What do we learn about him that helps us understand how he was able to accomplish all he did?

7. What was the underlying motivation for his acting with integrity and for his acts of compassion and justice for the poor?

8. What steps could you take to cultivate some of those same qualities in your life this week?

9. What actions could you and your fellowship group engage in this week that would develop and demonstrate those qualities?

Study 6: Systematic Relocation: a Human Investment
Nehemiah 7; 11:1-2

1. Read Nehemiah 7. What progress has Nehemiah made since we left him?

2. In verses 1-3, who is supposed to guard the city, and what are their instructions?

3. How is Hananiah described? What is meant by the words "a man of integrity [who] feared God more than most men do"?

4. What kinds of things must happen in your life before these words describe you?

5. Why was this quality important for his particular task?

6. At this point, how is the city described? Why was it like this (vv. 4-6)?

7. Verses 7-72 tell of Nehemiah's feeling the need to register the inhabitants by lineage, to connect the people with their heritage, and to define and regather the people of God who had been scattered in the exile. He chronicles all the transactions of the treasury in setting up their society. Twice, at the end of the chapter, Nehemiah mentions that people were not living inside the city walls but in their own nearby towns (vv. 73-74). Why does he do this? What is he concerned with?

8. When people make their living elsewhere than in the heart of the city, it's difficult to get them to want to live there. Yet getting people to live there is essential for the city's security and stability. It's the same in your city. The core of the city, the downtown area, will never come back to life unless people decide to invest in it.

9. Now jump to Nehemiah 11 and read verses 1-2. Why was it important for the leaders to do what they did? What was the effect in the rest of the community?

10. Why would a whole people make such an investment in the city? What kind of support was there for those who chose to go?

11. What would be the equivalent in your city today?

Study 7: Jesus' Heart of Compassion and Justice
Matthew 23:13-39; Luke 19:41-44

Background: Much of Jesus' ministry focused on the cities and communities of Israel (see, for example, Jn 2:13; 5:1; 7:14; 10:22-23; 12:12). As an integral part of that ministry, Jesus often goes into the city to engage its residents and then retreats to a quiet place to pray or teach the disciples. Jesus models a ministry that engages the city and then retreats to be refreshed. This pattern is most evident in the last week of Jesus' ministry before his death. Each day he entered the city to teach, and each evening he returned to Bethany. In this last week of ministry Jesus speaks against the injustices practiced by the Pharisees. At the same time his love for the ordinary people of Jerusalem is evident in his continual teaching and desire to be with them.

Before you study: Have you ever experienced or witnessed a clear injustice, something you instantly recognized was just downright wrong? For example, a friend of mine told me of accompanying a Hmong refugee to a social services office where the clerk, upon seeing the refugee, rolled her eyes and with disgust said, "Another one of you? How many more are there?" Or another example: Steve Morris, who is African-American and vice president of World Impact, shared about the time the checkout clerk accepted a check from the person in front of him with no ID, but required three IDs from him. Have you ever experienced something that really made you angry because you knew it was just wrong? How did you react?

1. Read Matthew 23:13-39. This section is partly broken up by seven "woes." Look at them and give each one a title.

2. Now define these sins using your own words. What was going on that Jesus was condemning?

3. What are some ways these things go on today? How do the injustices of the Pharisees compare with injustices that take place in the city today?

4. Jesus' tender prayer for Jerusalem in verses 37-39 is in striking contrast to his condemnation of the religious leaders of that city. Why do you think the tone changes so much from verse 33, "You snakes! You brood of vipers," to verse 37, "O Jerusalem, Jerusalem"?

5. How does Jesus describe Jerusalem in verse 37?

6. What word picture does he use to describe his love for the city of Jerusalem?

7. Why is he unable to act out his love?

8. What is the consequence of the people's unbelief (vv. 38-39)?

9. It's important to note that Jesus is constantly addressing the *religious* community concerning its involvement in the evils of the city. The unrighteous are virtually ignored. What lesson do you gain from Jesus' emphasis?

10. Read Luke 19:41-44. What was Jesus' reaction when he came near the city? Why did it affect him so much?

11. What does this tell us about Jesus?

12. Every day, as we read or watch the news, we see the pain of the city. What are the most recent examples in your city? Here are a few in mine:

☐ Our city has set a new record for murders. Uneducated and poor inner-city youth, fourth- and fifth-graders, are carrying guns to settle differences.

☐ About 25 percent of the people in our city, which is located in an area with America's largest agricultural economy (nearly three billion dollars annually), live below the federally established poverty level.

☐ The rich get immediate attention in court when they get into trouble, while the poor wait in jail often for months to see an overworked public defender.

Jesus could visualize the imminent destruction of a city whose people reject their Lord (Luke 19:43). He felt the pain of this tragic situation enough to cry. He let it affect him.

In light of all this, perhaps the most important question we can ask ourselves is: *Why don't we weep over our city as Jesus wept over his?*

13. Share with someone else, as honestly as you can, why you don't want to look closely at the evil of your city. Why is it all too easy to look the other way? (Is one reason that if you look too closely at the problems you might feel compelled to *do* something?)

Study 8: Fly Like a Dove or Call on the Lord?
Psalm 55:9-11, 4-8, 16-18, 22.

1. Read Psalm 55:9-11. How does the psalmist describe the city? What are some of the key words he uses?

2. What are some examples in your city of
☐ ruin
☐ malice
☐ violence
☐ strife
☐ oppression
☐ fraud

3. Read verses 4-8. What is the psalmist's response to what he sees? What does it make him want to do?

4. What kinds of things do we do to avoid the problems of the city? How do those problems make you feel?

5. Read verses 16-18. What does he finally do instead?

6. Read verse 22. How does calling on the Lord affect him?

7. The psalmist could move ahead in living out God's agenda for his life only in a *spirit of dependence* on God. Otherwise, the problems of the city would be overwhelming. That is what must characterize our approach to ministry in the city. What step can you take this week to cultivate a spirit of dependence on the Lord?

Study 9: A Spiritual Life That Really Pleases God
Isaiah 58:1-14

Background: Fasting is a time of self-denial and repentance for sin. After the fall of Jerusalem the number of fast days increased, but that was no guarantee the people's hearts would be repentant over personal or national sins. Fasting and pious activity in general, without corresponding humility of heart before God, are nothing but hypocrisy. It is to this attitude that God speaks powerfully in this passage.

Before you study: Imagine your church or fellowship group being described as
☐ seeming eager to know God's ways
☐ asking God for just decisions in their lives
☐ seeming eager for God to come near
☐ humbling themselves before God

It would be easy to feel as if your ministry were mature, successful and complete, wouldn't it?

1. Read Isaiah 58:1-5. How was Israel expressing its spirituality? Why wasn't God pleased?

2. What is behind the false piety of keeping fast days while doing things contrary to the Lord's concerns for people?

3. What are some examples of this happening in your life or the life of your church?

4. Read verses 6-14. What are the specific elements of God's idea of true piety? Write them down.

5. What values do they reflect? Write them down.

6. What are the benefits listed for keeping his kind of "fast"? Write them down.

7. How might non-Christian people react if the church radically committed itself to the kind of fasting God outlines in this passage?

8. What might you do this week to obey at least one of the values and corresponding actions you see in Isaiah 58?

Study 10: Evidence of Saving Faith
James 1:26—2:17

Background: Many parts of the book of James echo with the words of the author's brother Jesus. (Compare 5:1-3 with Mt 6:19, for example.) It's no surprise, then, that James champions the cause of the poor, those to whom Jesus spent so much of his time ministering.

1. Read James 1:26—2:17. What does James consider the characteristics of people who would call themselves "religious"?

2. Why would James summarize the Christian faith in such a stark, behavior-oriented way? Why not just say, "Religion that our God and Father accepts is when people accept Jesus into their heart"?

3. Jesus said that we would do the works he was doing (Jn 14:12). Psalm 146:7-9 describes God as being one who watches over the fatherless and the widow, one who gives food to the hungry, one who sets prisoners free, one who gives sight to the blind and so on. These words sound a lot like Jesus' mission as he described it in Luke 4. James, by using similar language, is suggesting that the very nature of religious faith is that it must express itself in selfless acts on behalf of those who are in need. What is the conclusion of this passage regarding a "faith" or

"religion" that is *not* characterized by these things?

4. In what way is the teaching on favoritism in this passage an example of the previous point?

5. In 2:8 James centers his teaching on faith in the doctrine of neighbor-love. Again, we can hear the sound of his brother Jesus' voice as he taught the parable of the good Samaritan, who crossed ethnic barriers and showed a costly love of neighbor. Our world is urbanizing at an amazing rate; the peoples of the world are moving into the neighborhood, and opportunities will abound to demonstrate the relevance of the gospel. But what kind of gospel will we represent? What kind does James want us to represent?

6. James brings the truth home hard. "Faith without works is dead." What might be the telltale signs that someone's faith is becoming only a matter of words—"beliefs" without corresponding actions?

7. What are some things that friends in Christ could do to help each other assess where they are in this process?

Study 11: Location, Location, Location
Jeremiah 32:1-15

Background: Jeremiah is in prison for speaking the unpleasant word of God to his nation. Babylon is on the doorsteps of the city, ready to deal the final blow. The nation is only months away from being carted off into captivity, exiled from their homeland for many generations. In the midst of this, a distant cousin comes to Jeremiah in prison and wants him to exercise his option to buy a piece of land. Hanamel must know that now is not a good time to own land, since the market is pretty depressed over the coming invasion. He wants out, preferring cash in his pocket, and apparently not feeling too bad about hitting up Jeremiah in jail. (This guy has to receive an F for sensitivity.)

1. Read Jeremiah 32:1-15. How would you have felt if you were in Jeremiah's shoes, not only being used by your cousin but being commanded by God to do something that seemed so foolish?

2. How does Jeremiah respond instead? Why is he able to do this?

3. Why would the Lord want Jeremiah to invest in land that is nearly

worthless and is going to be captured any day? What was this action meant to communicate?

4. What was behind the elaborate transfer of title that the Lord had Jeremiah arrange (why such a public transfer, with such care taken to preserve the arrangement with methods that would last a long time)? What was the nation supposed to learn from this?

5. Are there areas in your city that the real estate industry has labeled "somewhere you wouldn't want to buy"? Are there areas which the banks seldom write loans for? Would God ask his people to invest in such a risky place? What would be his reason?

6. Would you ever consider making such a "poor" investment? What kinds of things would hold you back? How would your friends and family respond if you moved in that direction? How would you explain your reasons to them if God should call you in that direction?

7. If the real estate industry uses the mantra "Location, Location, Location" as its criterion for making a purchase, what should be the criterion for a Christian in deciding where to live? Is this decision connected to personal discipleship, or is it just part of everyday life? Explain.

Appendix 2

21 Things You Can Do to Love the City
These are steps you can take alone, with a friend, with your family or with a group at church or on campus.

1. Take a drive through a poor section of town. See if you can keep track of a few things and compare them to your neighborhood.

☐ Count the boarded-up houses and houses for sale.

☐ Count the number of supermarkets or food chains.

☐ Measure the ratio of check-cashing stores and currency exchanges to banks.

☐ Note the condition of the streets, the amount of graffiti, the state of repair of the sidewalks.

☐ See how many different ethnic-specific restaurants you can identify.

2. Ask an inner-city church if they will sponsor an urban tour for you and some friends so you can learn about the needs of that part of the city. They know their neighborhoods and can give you more background and history than you would have access to on your own.

3. Attend an inner-city church that is ethnically different from you. Hang around long enough to be greeted afterward. You may even be invited over for lunch.

4. Sign up with an inner-city school or church to help with their

after-school clubs or tutoring programs.

5. Walk a child home after the tutoring program and see where he or she lives. Meet the parent or parents if you can.

6. Be a big brother or big sister to an inner-city child or teen. Take him or her with you on outings or visits to your family.

7. Sign up with a local men's or women's shelter to serve in their soup kitchen or clothing room once a week.

8. Contact a campus ministry at the nearest university to see if they have an urban program which you could support.

9. Find out what the Bible has to say about God's love for the city, for the poor and oppressed. (see Appendix 1.)

10. Sponsor a joint youth group service project (paint, build a house with Habitat for Humanity, pick up trash) connecting a suburban church group with an inner-city church group.

11. Invite the choir of an inner-city church of a different ethnicity than yours to come to your church. Take your choir to their church, if they want you. Trade pastors once or twice a year.

12. Attend a downtown cultural festival where you can sample the different foods and appreciate the artistic and musical presentations represented.

13. Spend a night with a family that lives in a neglected neighborhood. Arrange it through your church.

14. Get together with friends and do a prayer walk through a neglected neighborhood. Do it with residents of that area if possible. Try it weekly for a month.

15. Get an apartment with friends or with another couple in the heart of a needy neighborhood, and live there for six months.

16. Attend a meeting of the neighborhood revitalization department of your local government. See what the hottest issues are. How might the gospel speak to these needs?

17. Ask a representative of the police to come and speak to your Sunday-school class. Ask what churches can do to help heal broken neighborhoods.

18. Read a book about ministry in the city. (See suggestions on p. 144.)

19. Join a weekly outreach to youth in your city's juvenile hall (e.g., Youth for Christ's Youth Guidance Division or a church's weekly ministry). Keep contact with those you meet after they are released.

20. Price your favorite foods at your supermarket or price club, then go to a corner market in the inner city. Price them there and compare. Ask yourself the implications of the difference and whether this has any bearing on why the poor are poor.

21. Pray that God will show you how to discern what he is calling you to do—how he wants you to respond to the needs and opportunities of the city.

Notes

Chapter One: Flying Upside Down
[1]1990 Fresno County Census.
[2]Ibid.
[3]Juan Carlos Ortiz, *Disciple* (Wheaton, Ill.: Creation House, 1975), p. 15.
[4]Robert C. Linthicum, *City of God, City of Satan: A Biblical Theology for the Urban Church* (Grand Rapids, Mich.: Zondervan, 1991), p. 102.
[5]Ibid., p. 100.

Chapter Two: This Old House
[1]Rodney Clapp, *Families at the Crossroads* (Downers Grove, Ill.: InterVarsity Press, 1993), p. 156.
[2]Ibid., p. 163.

Chapter Three: Behold the City
[1]Attributed to Marcel Post, although I cannot find the source.
[2]William Penn, *Reflections and Maxims,* publisher and date unknown.
[3]Linthicum, *City of God, City of Satan,* p. 29.
[4]H. Richard Niebuhr, *Christ and Culture* (New York: HarperCollins, 1956).
[5]James Westgate, in a lecture on urban mission, Fresno, Calif., 1993.
[6]Ray Bakke, *The Urban Christian* (Downers Grove, Ill.: InterVarsity Press, 1987), p. 62.
[7]James Westgate, *Urban Theology,* unpublished doctoral dissertation.
[8]Bakke, *Urban Christian,* p. 68.
[9]Westgate, *Urban Theology,* p. 49.
[10]Tom Sine, *The Mustard Seed Conspiracy* (Waco, Tex.: Word, 1981), p. 78.
[11]Harvie M. Conn, *A Clarified Vision for Urban Mission* (Grand Rapids, Mich.:

Zondervan, 1987), p. 44.

[12]Tim Hackler, "The Big City Has No Corner on Mental Illness," *New York Times Magazine*, December 19, 1979, pp. 136, 138.

[13]Conn, *A Clarified Vision*, p. 45.

Chapter Four: Love Thy Neighborhood

[1]Craig S. Keener, *The IVP Bible Background Commentary: New Testament* (Downers Grove, Ill.: InterVarsity Press, 1993), p. 218.

[2]Robert D. Lupton, *Theirs Is the Kingdom: Celebrating the Gospel in Urban America* (San Francisco: Harper, 1989), p. 37.

Chapter Five: What's Good for the Goose . . .

[1]James T. Burtchaell, quoted in Clapp, *Families at the Crossroads*, p. 149.

[2]Allan Bloom, *The Closing of the American Mind* (New York: Simon & Schuster/Touchstone, 1988), p. 59.

[3]Ibid., p. 58.

[4]Attributed to Marian Wright Edelman, president of the Children's Defense Fund.

[5]Amelia Earhart, quoted in *Columbia Dictionary of Quotations* (New York: Columbia University Press, 1993), p. 190.

Chapter Six: Like Working a Loom

[1]Robert D. Lupton, *Return Flight* (Atlanta, Ga.: FCS Urban Ministries, 1993), p. 21.

[2]Ronald J. Sider, *Rich Christians in an Age of Hunger* (Downers Grove, Ill.: InterVarsity Press, 1977), p. 88.

[3]Ibid., p. 89.

[4]Ibid., p. 223.

[5]Ibid.

[6]Lupton, *Return Flight*, p. 18.

[7]*Return Flight* is the title of Bob Lupton's book that describes the concept of Christian community development in detail (see note 1 above).

[8]Lupton, *Return Flight*, p. 48.

[9]Ibid., p. 68.

[10]John J. Palen, *The Urban World* (New York: McGraw Hill, 1987), p. 113.

[11]Ibid., p. 5.

[12]Ibid., p. 3.

[13]This concept attributed to H Spees, director of Fresno/Madera Youth for Christ.

[14]Eugene Peterson, *The Message* (Colorado Springs, Colo.: NavPress, 1992). A paraphrase of the New Testament which is both faithful to the Greek text and designed to speak God's Word to the American ear.

Epilogue: Journey of a Thousand Miles

[1]Robert Boyd Munger, *My Heart—Christ's Home* (Downers Grove, Ill.: InterVarsity Press, 1954, 1986).

Bibliography

Bakke, Ray. *The Urban Christian.* Downers Grove, Ill.: InterVarsity Press, 1987.

Claerbaut, David. *Urban Ministry.* Grand Rapids, Mich.: Zondervan, 1983.

Conn, Harvie. *A Clarified Vision for Urban Mission.* Grand Rapids, Mich.: Zondervan, 1987.

Dawson, John. *Taking Our Cities for God.* Lake Mary, Fla.: Creation House, 1989.

Duncan, Michael. *Costly Mission.* Monrovia, Calif.: MARC Publications, 1996.

Elliott, Clifford A. S. *Speaking for Themselves.* Toronto: United Church Publishing House, 1990.

Ellison, Craig W., and Edward S. Maynard. *Healing for the City.* Grand Rapids, Mich.: Zondervan, 1992.

Greenway, Roger S., and Timothy M. Monsma. *Cities: Missions' New Frontier.* Grand Rapids, Mich.: Baker, 1989.

Greenway, Roger S., ed. *Discipling the City.* Grand Rapids, Mich.: Baker, 1992.

Grigg, Viv. *Cry of the Urban Poor.* Monrovia, Calif.: MARC Publications, 1992.

Linthicum, Robert C. *City of God, City of Satan.* Grand Rapids, Mich.: Zondervan, 1991.

Lupton, Robert D. *Return Flight.* Atlanta, Ga.: FCS Urban Ministries, 1993.

_____. *Theirs Is the Kingdom.* San Francisco: Harper, 1989.

McClung, Floyd. *Seeing the City with the Eyes of God.* Tarrytown, N.Y.: Chosen Books, 1991.

Meyers, Eleanor Scott. *Envisioning the New City.* Louisville, Ky.: Westminster/John Knox, 1992.

Palen, John J. *The Urban World.* New York: McGraw Hill, 1987.

Perkins, John M. *A Quiet Revolution.* Waco, Tex.: Word, 1976.

_____. *Restoring At-Risk Communities.* Grand Rapids, Mich.: Baker, 1995.

_____. *Resurrecting Hope.* Ventura, Calif.: Regal, 1995.

Phillips, Keith. *No Quick Fix.* Ventura, Calif.: Regal, 1985.

Schlossberg, Herbert, Pierra Berthoud, Clark H. Pinnock and Marvin Olasky, ed. *Freedom, Justice and Hope.* Westchester, Ill.: Crossway, 1988.

Sider, Ronald J. *Cup of Water, Bread of Life.* Grand Rapids, Mich.: Zondervan, 1994.